MW01537837

This Coloring Book Belongs to ....

....

....

....

....

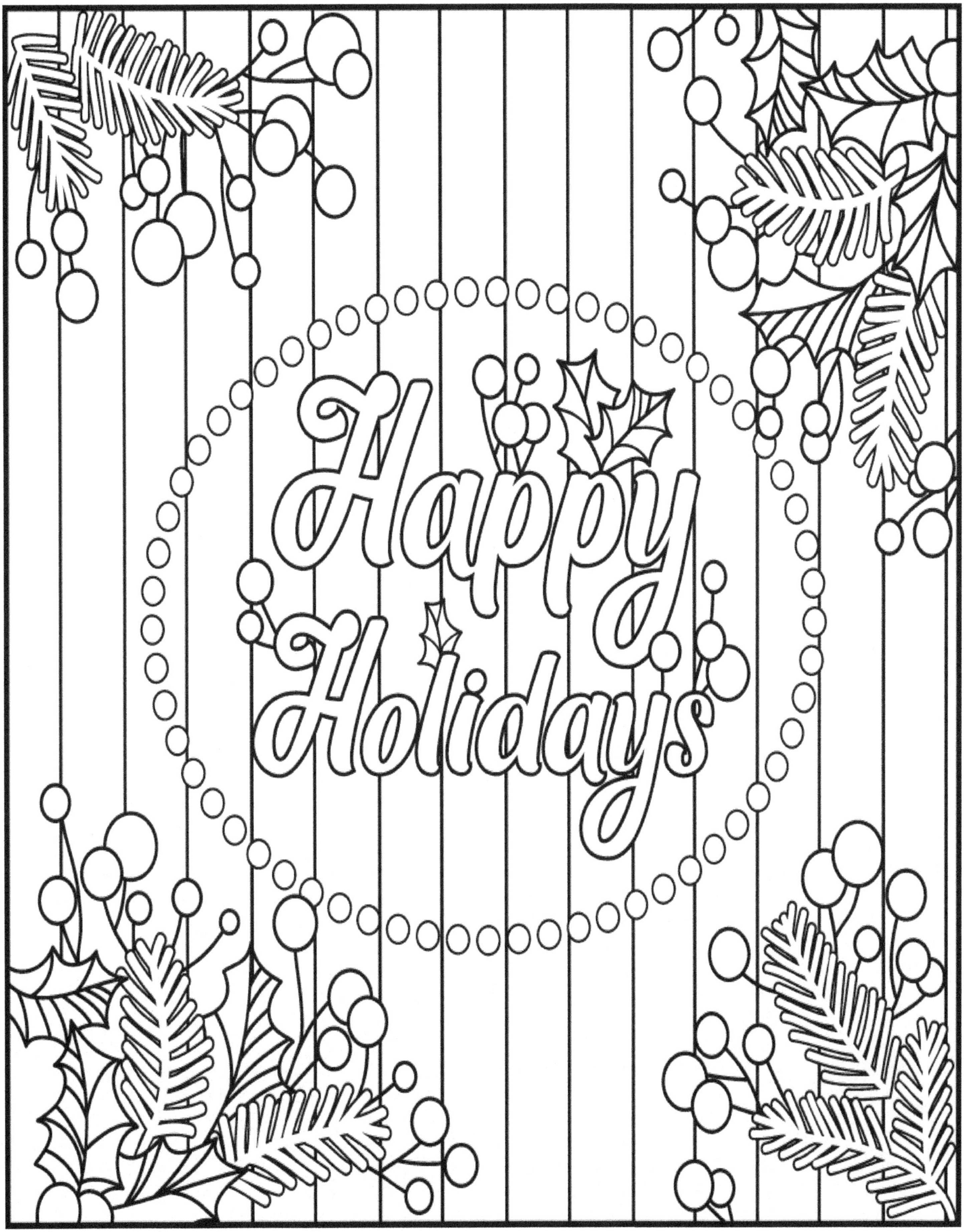
Happy
Holidays

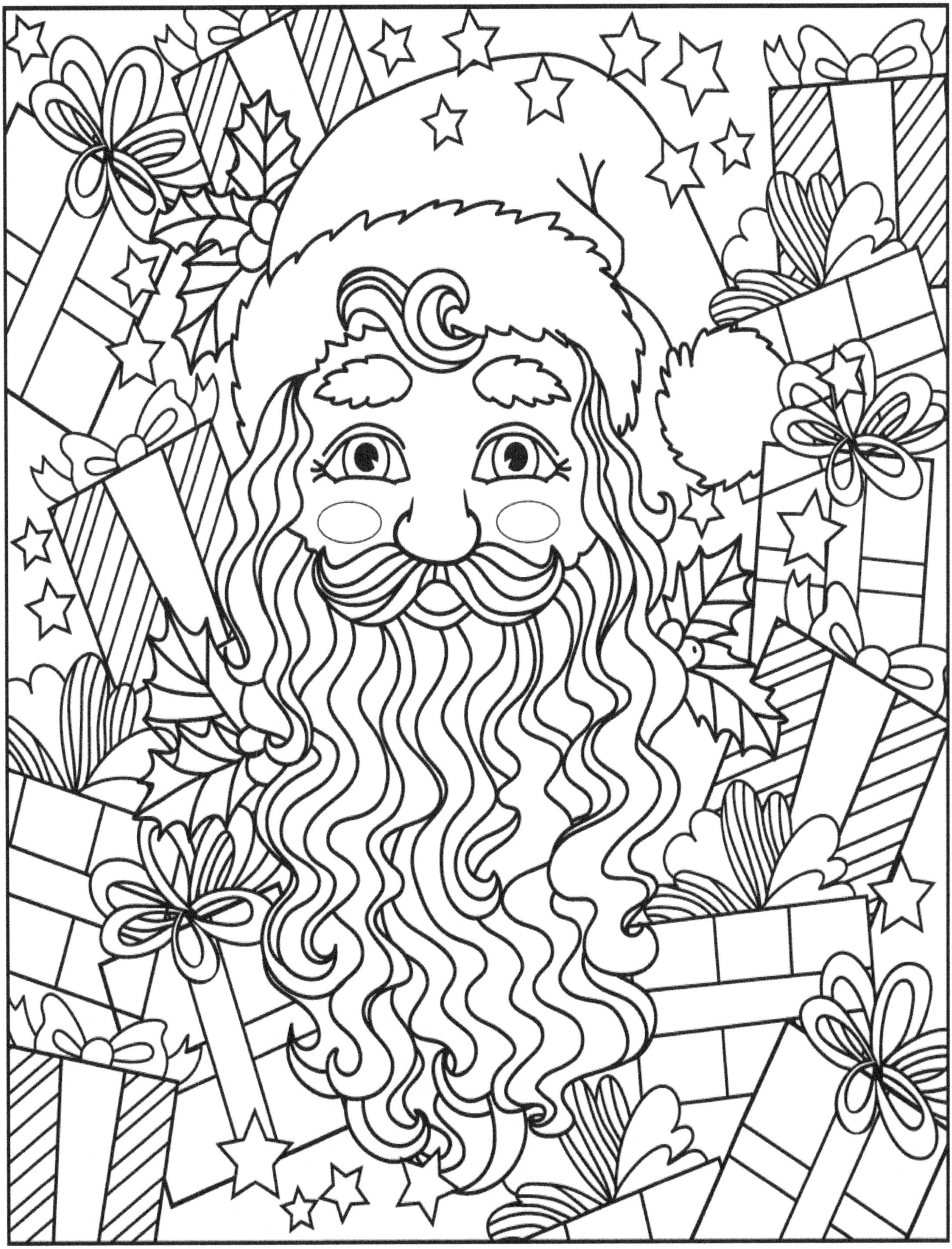

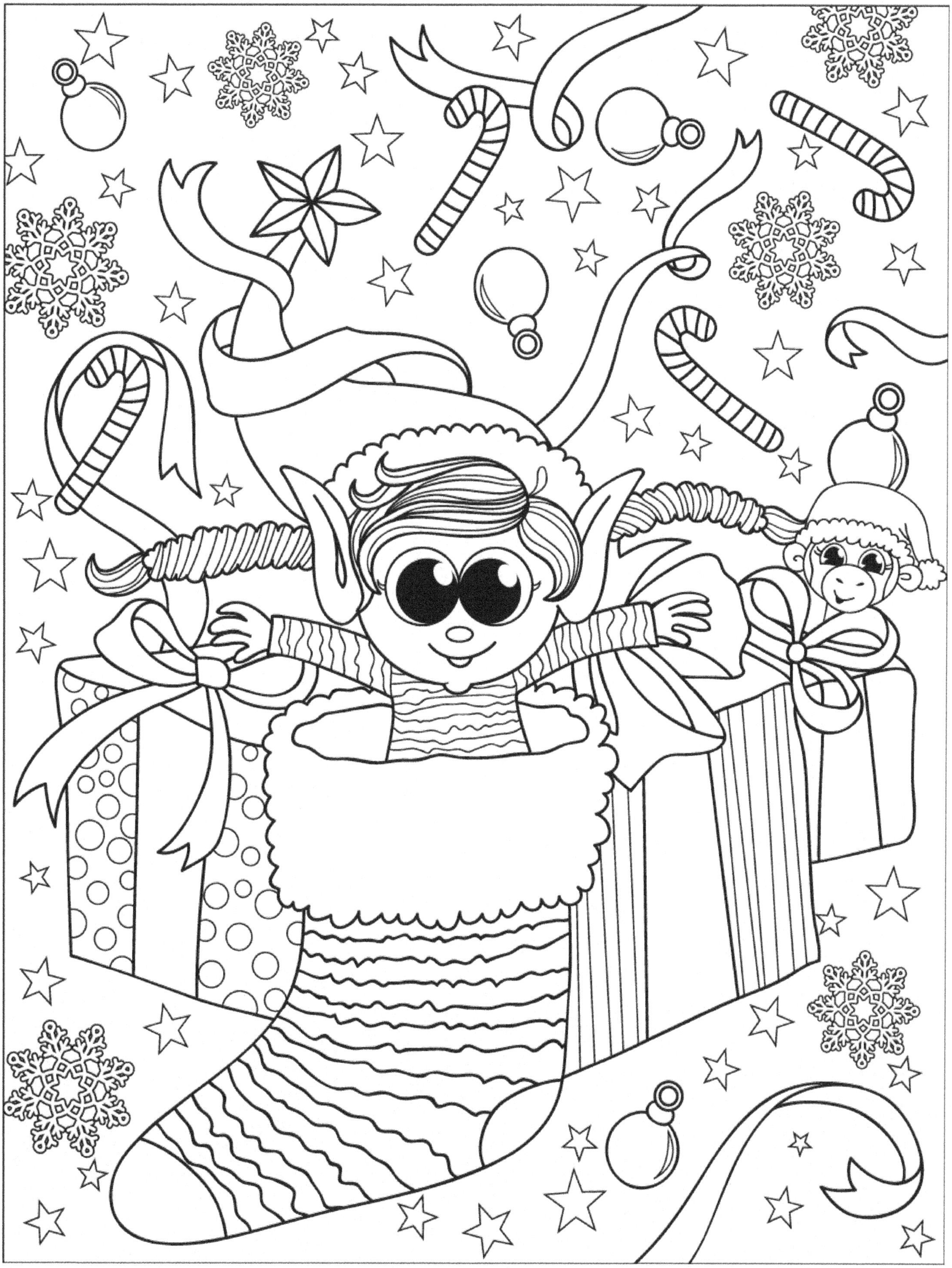

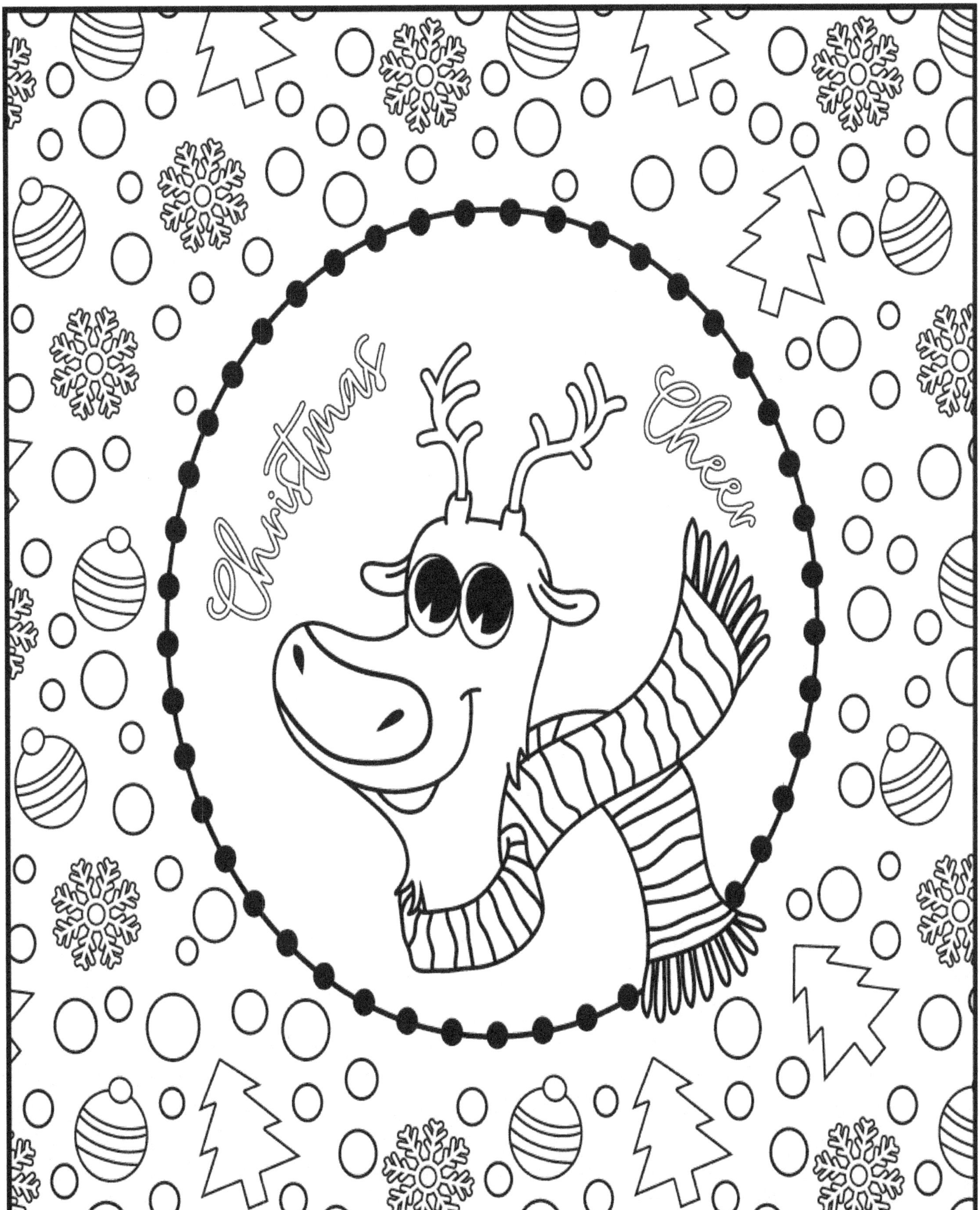
Christmas
Cheer

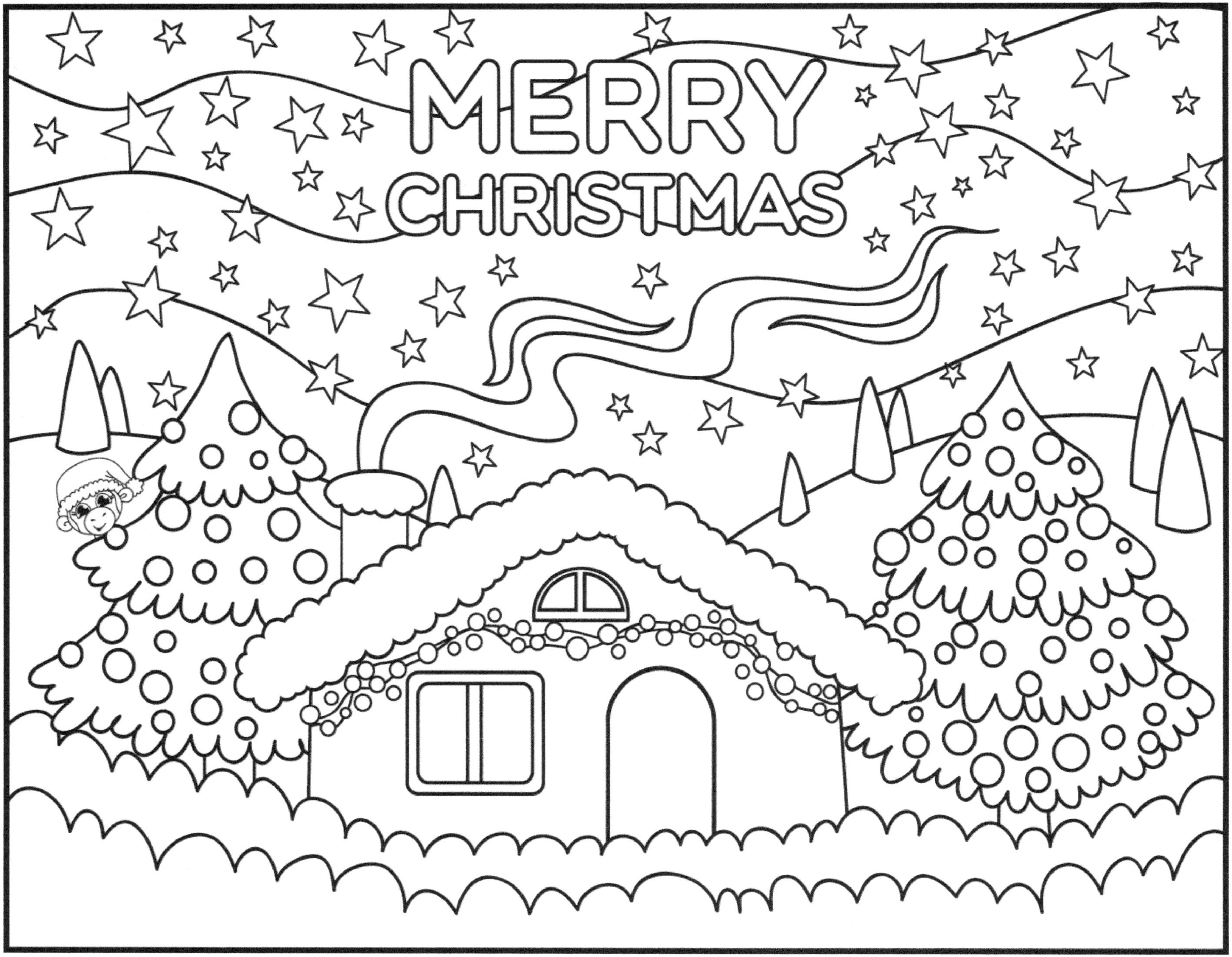
MERRY
CHRISTMAS

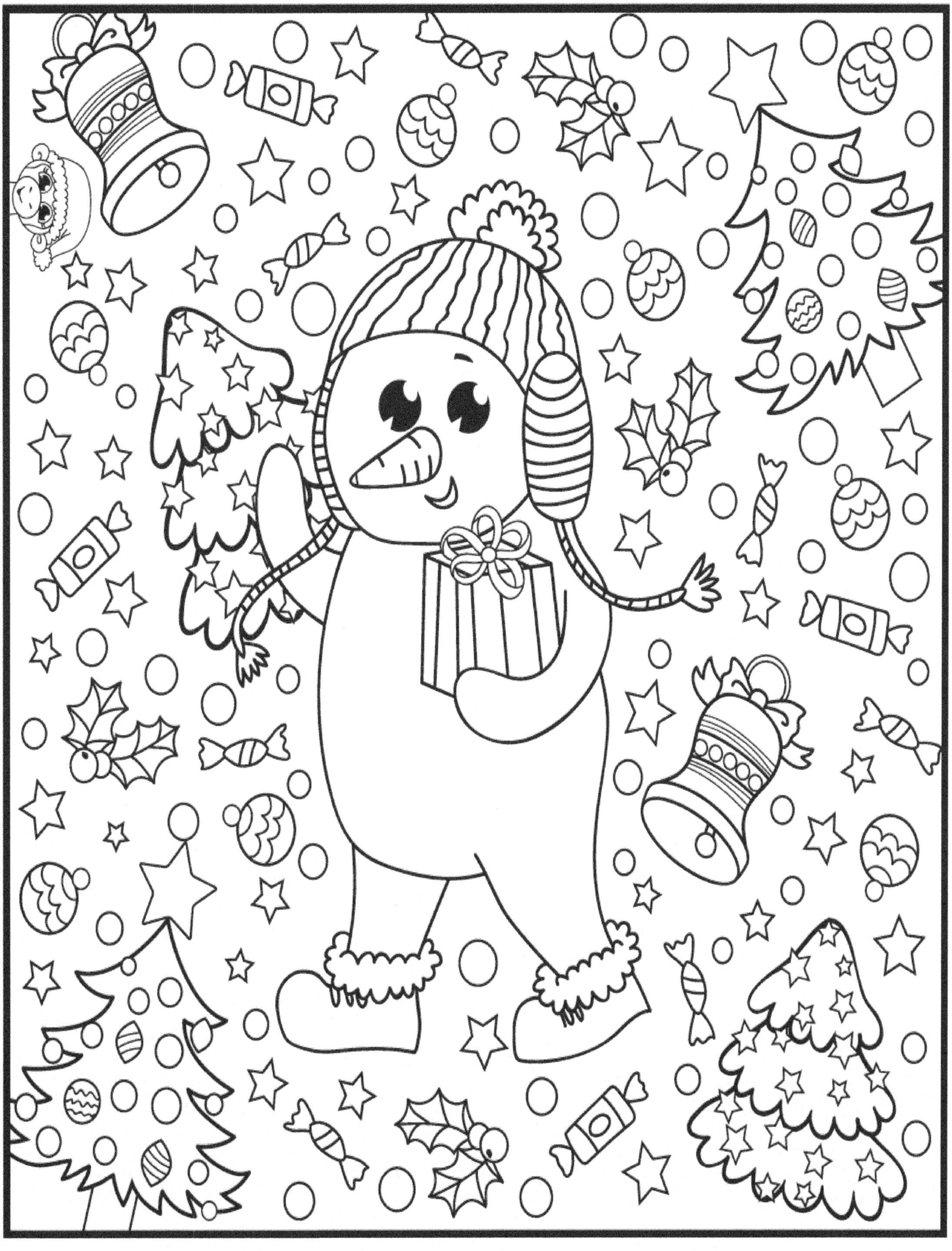

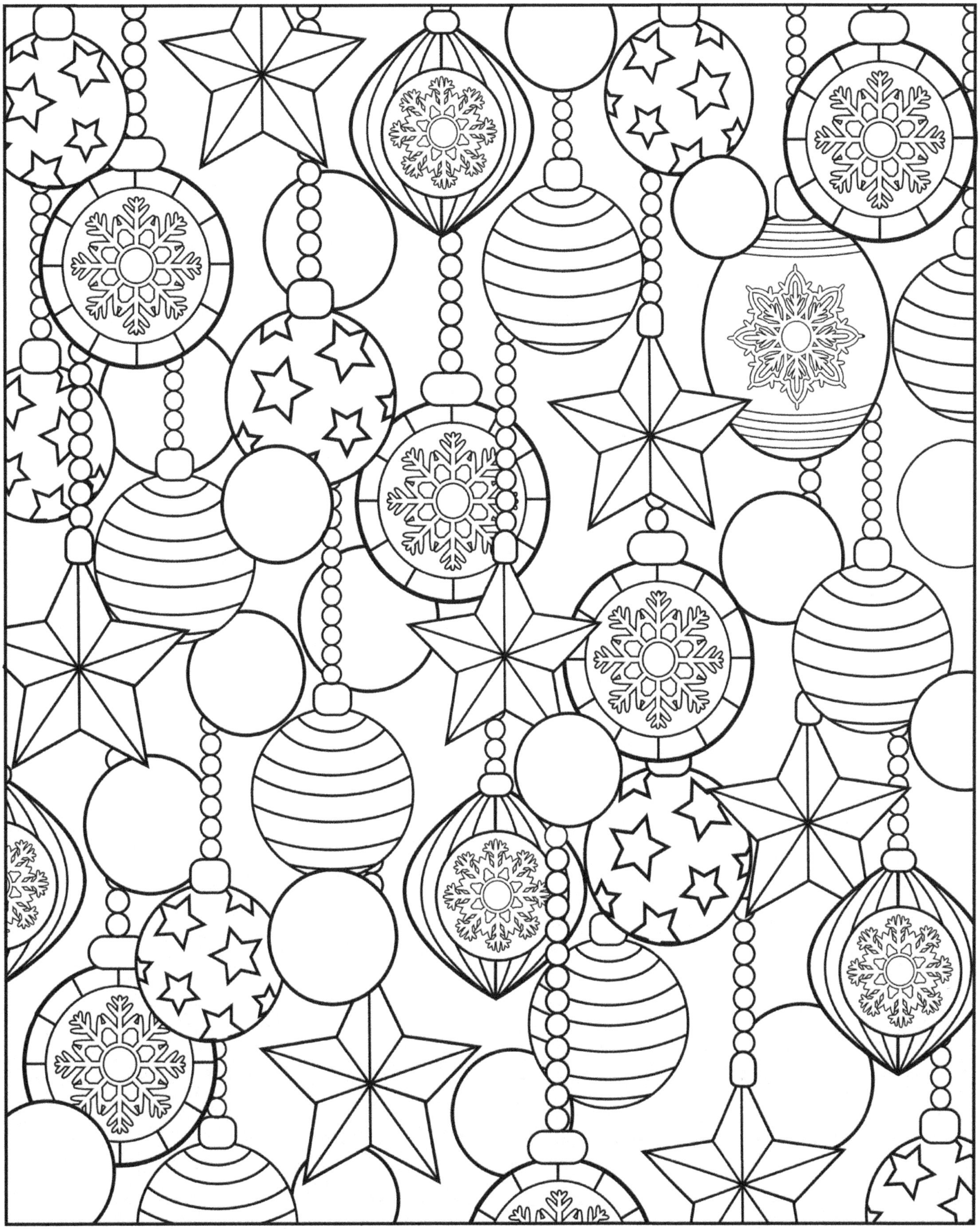

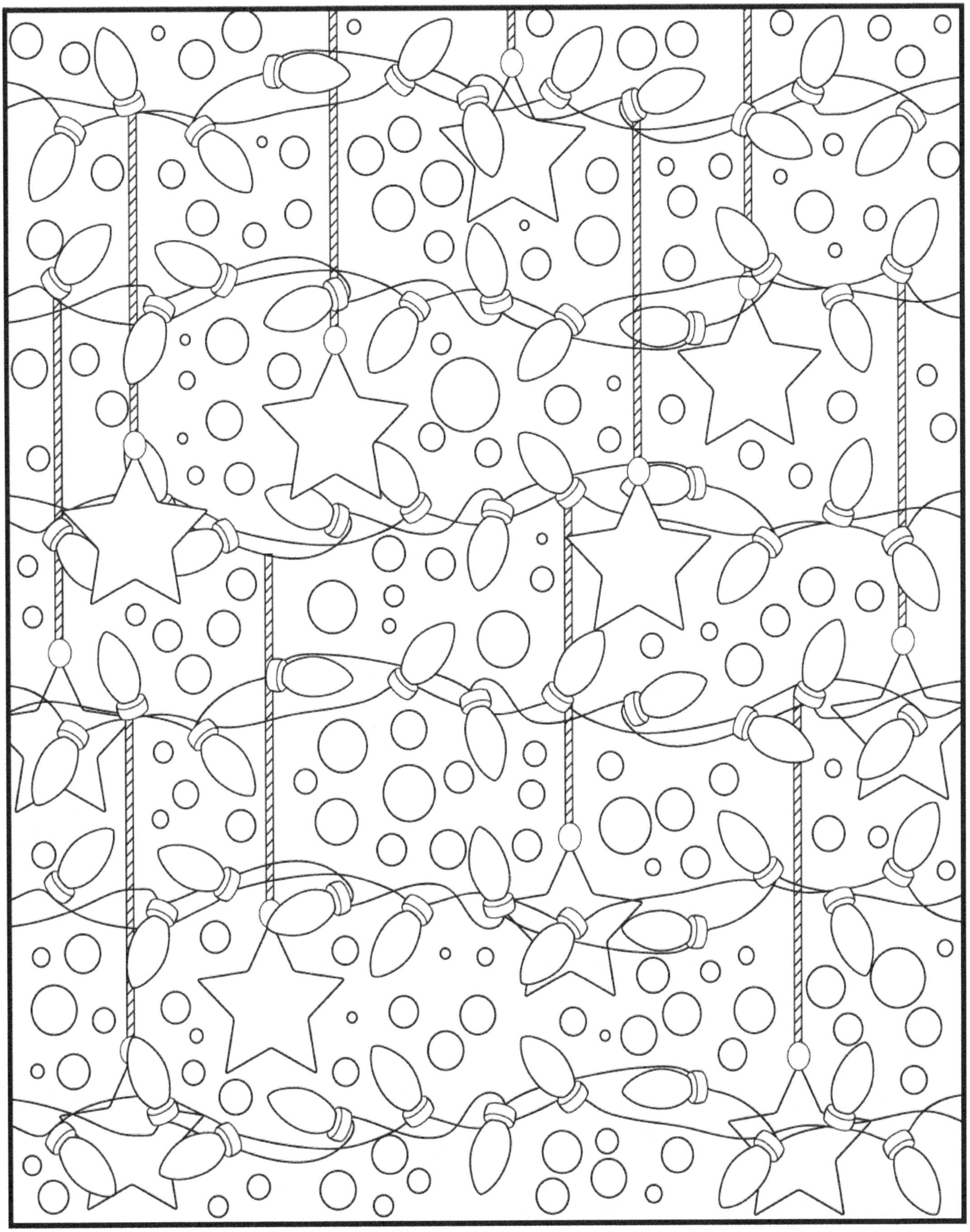

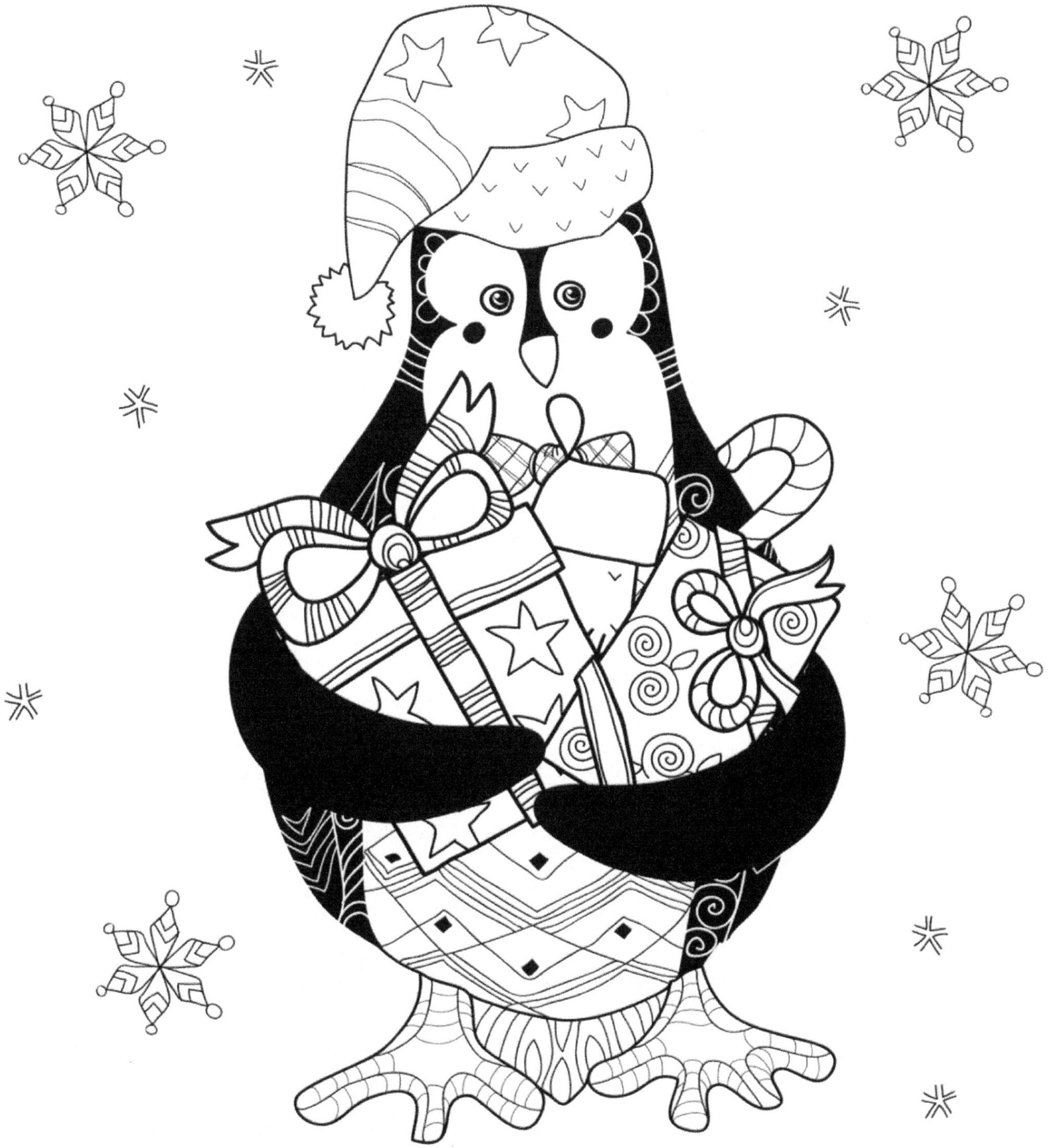

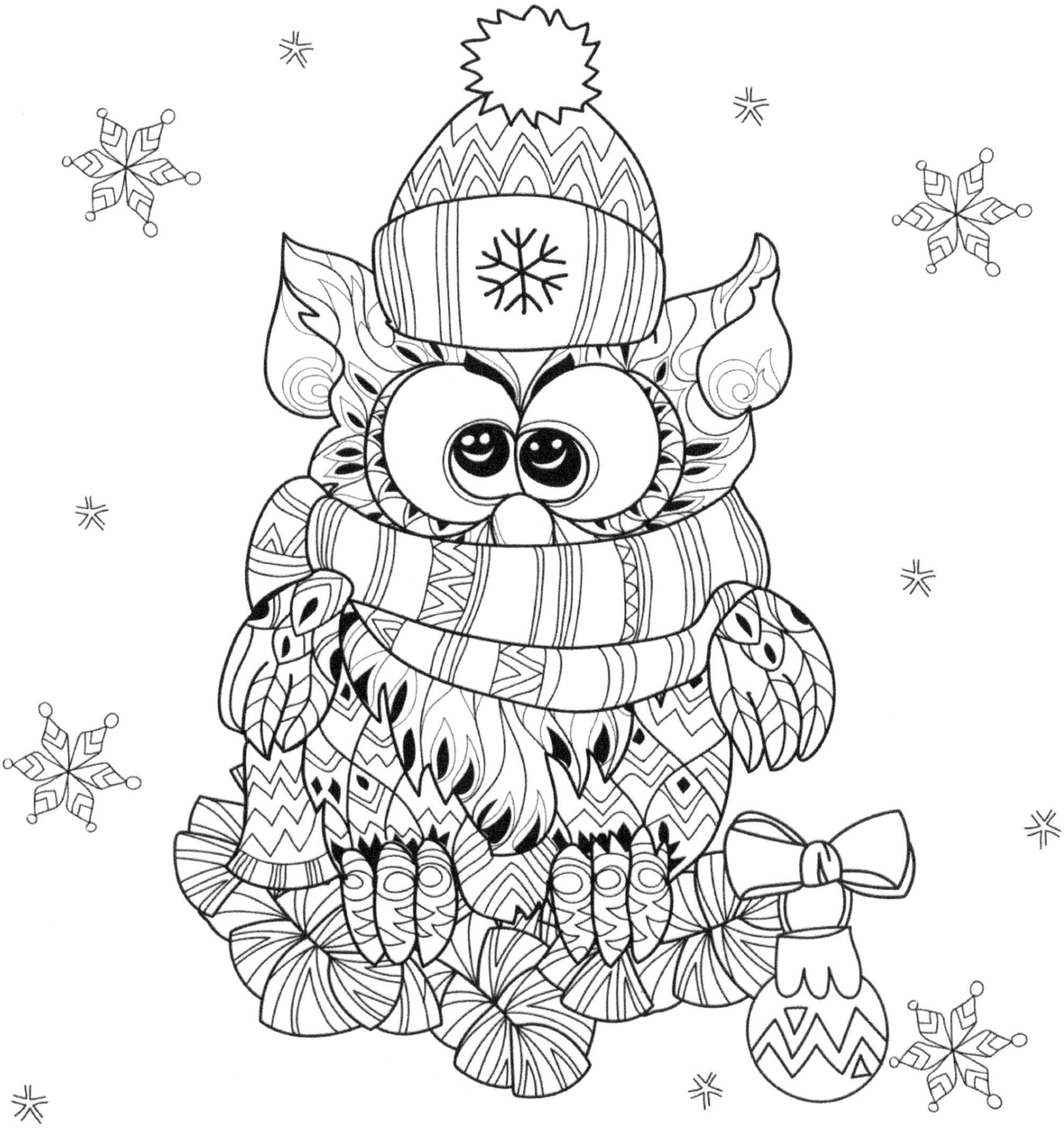

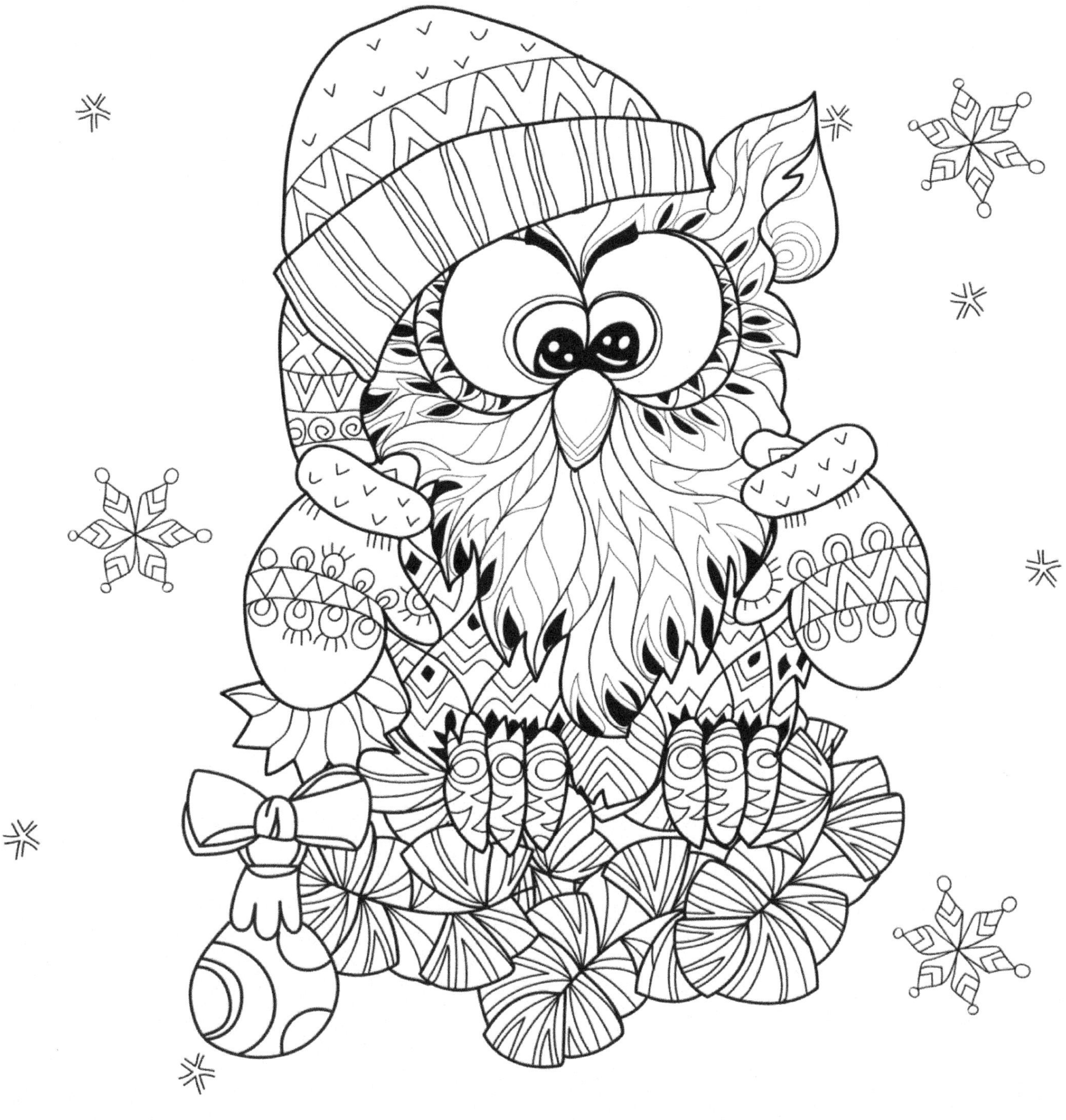

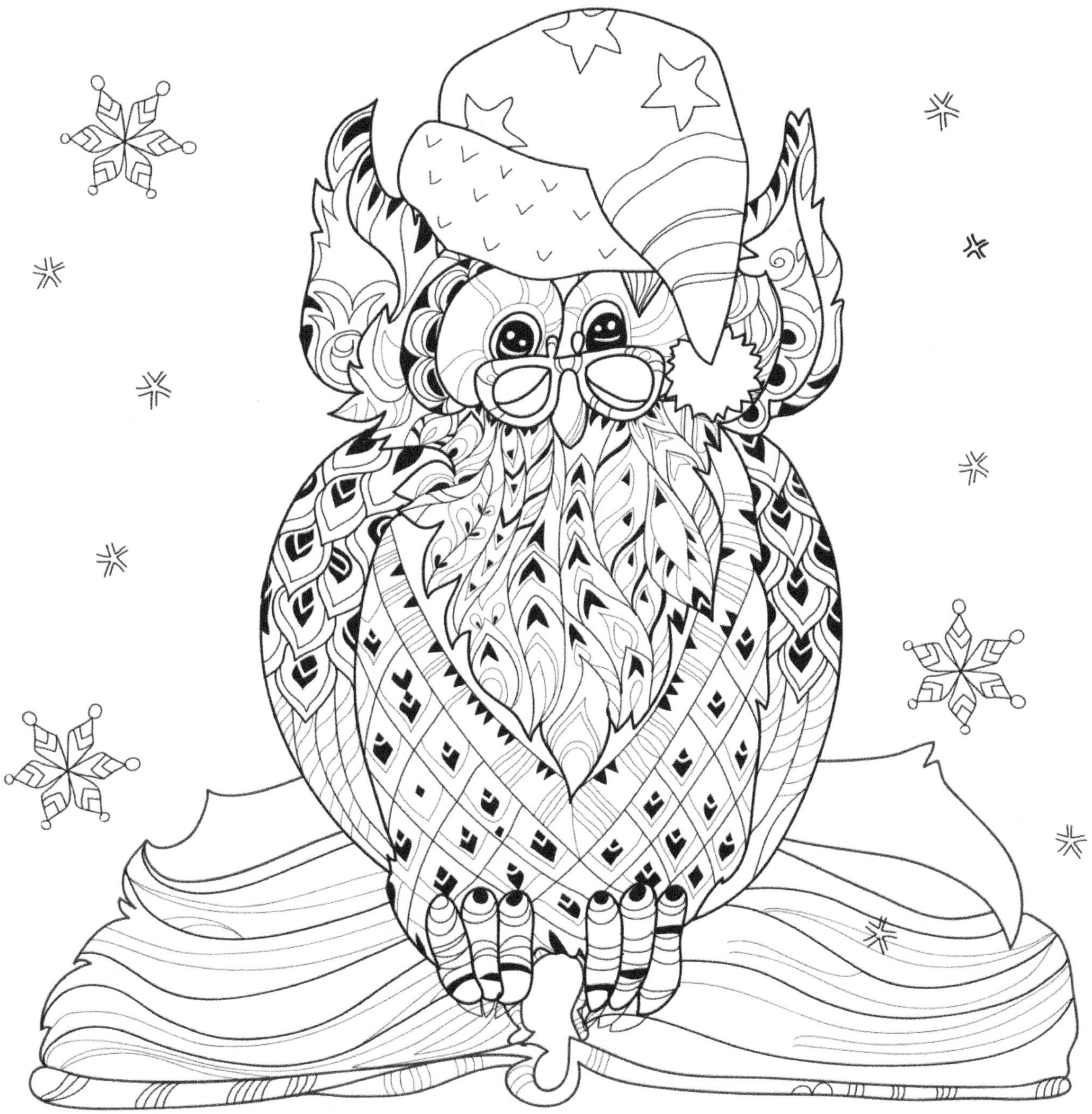

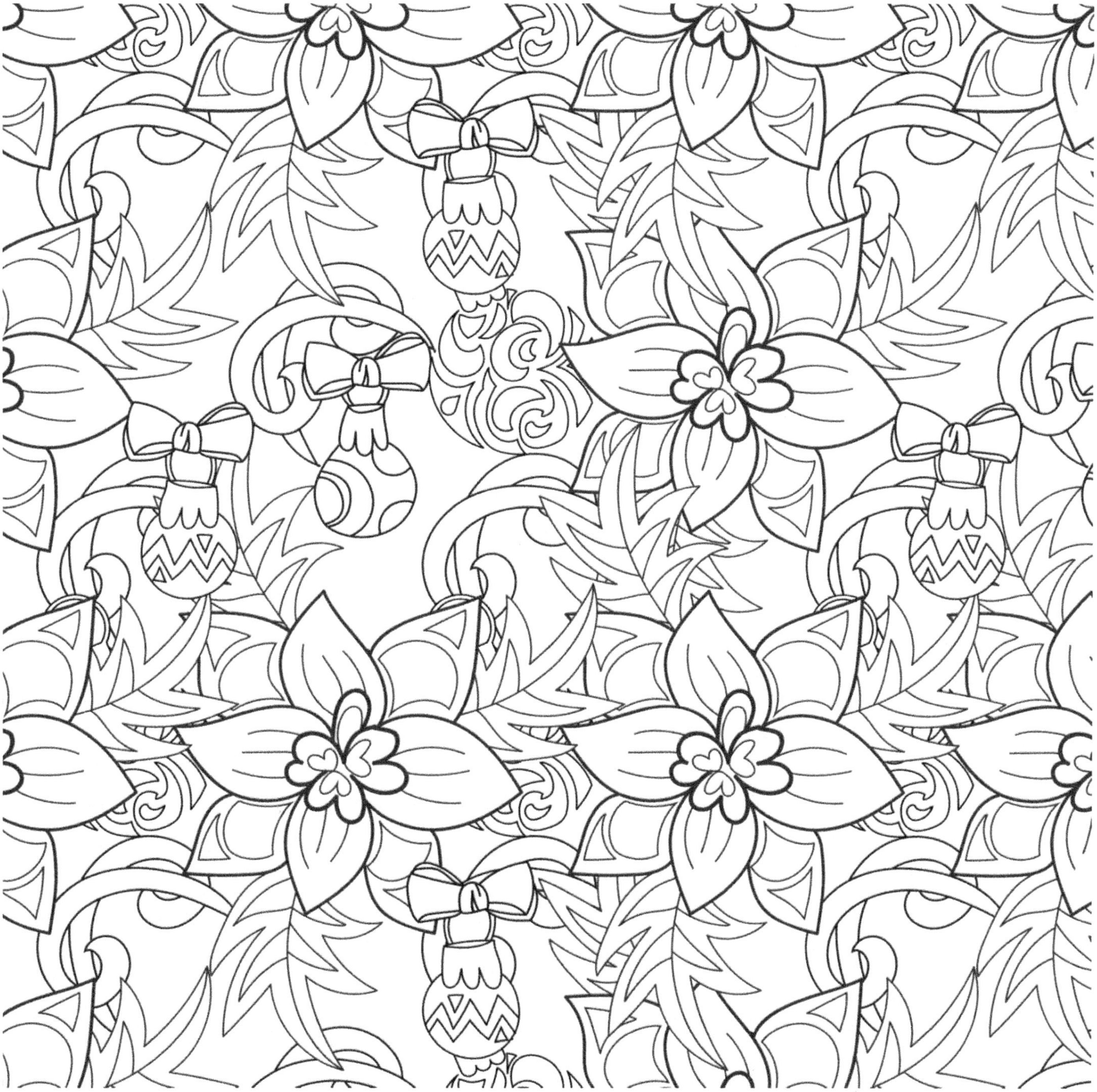

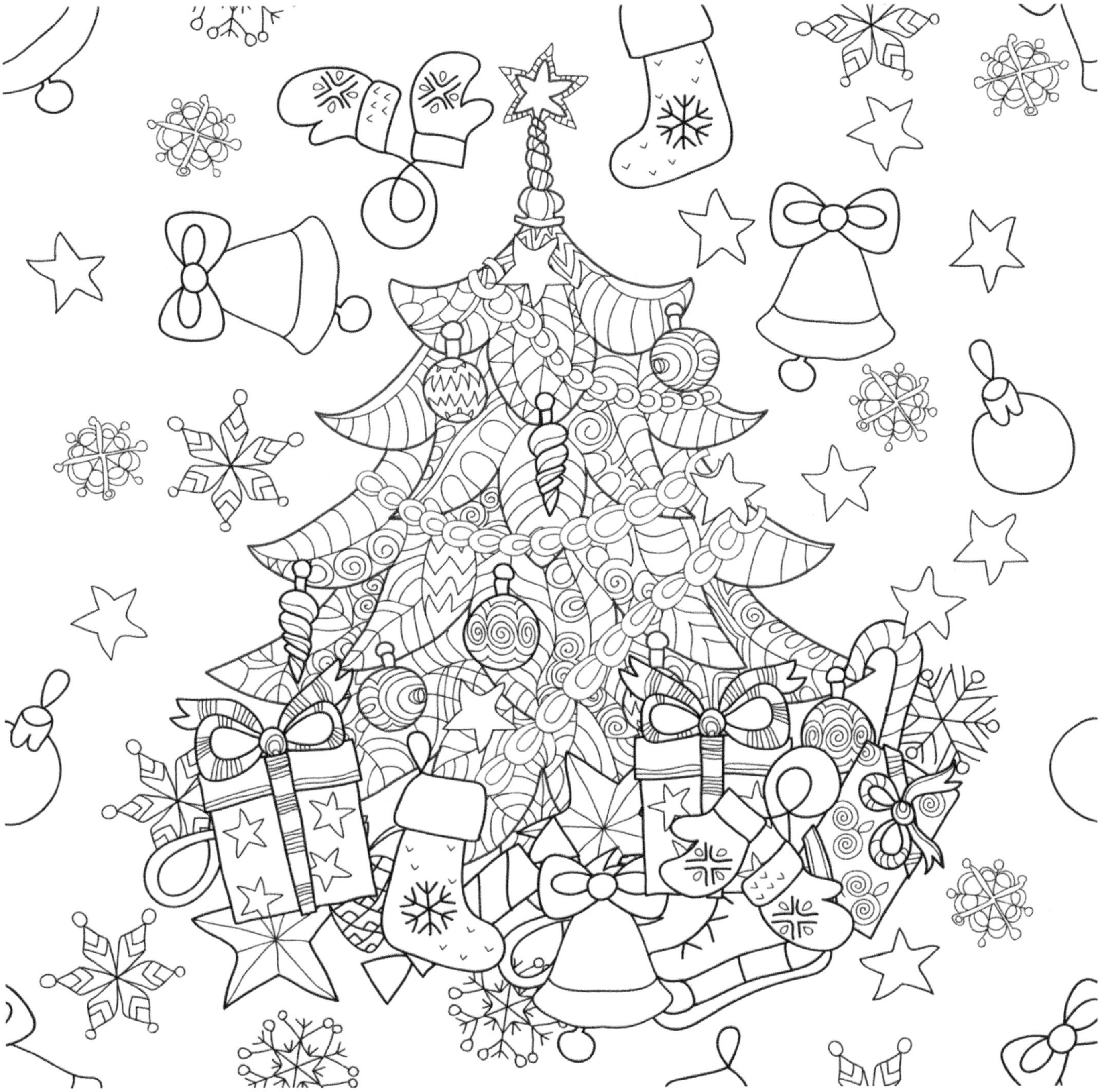

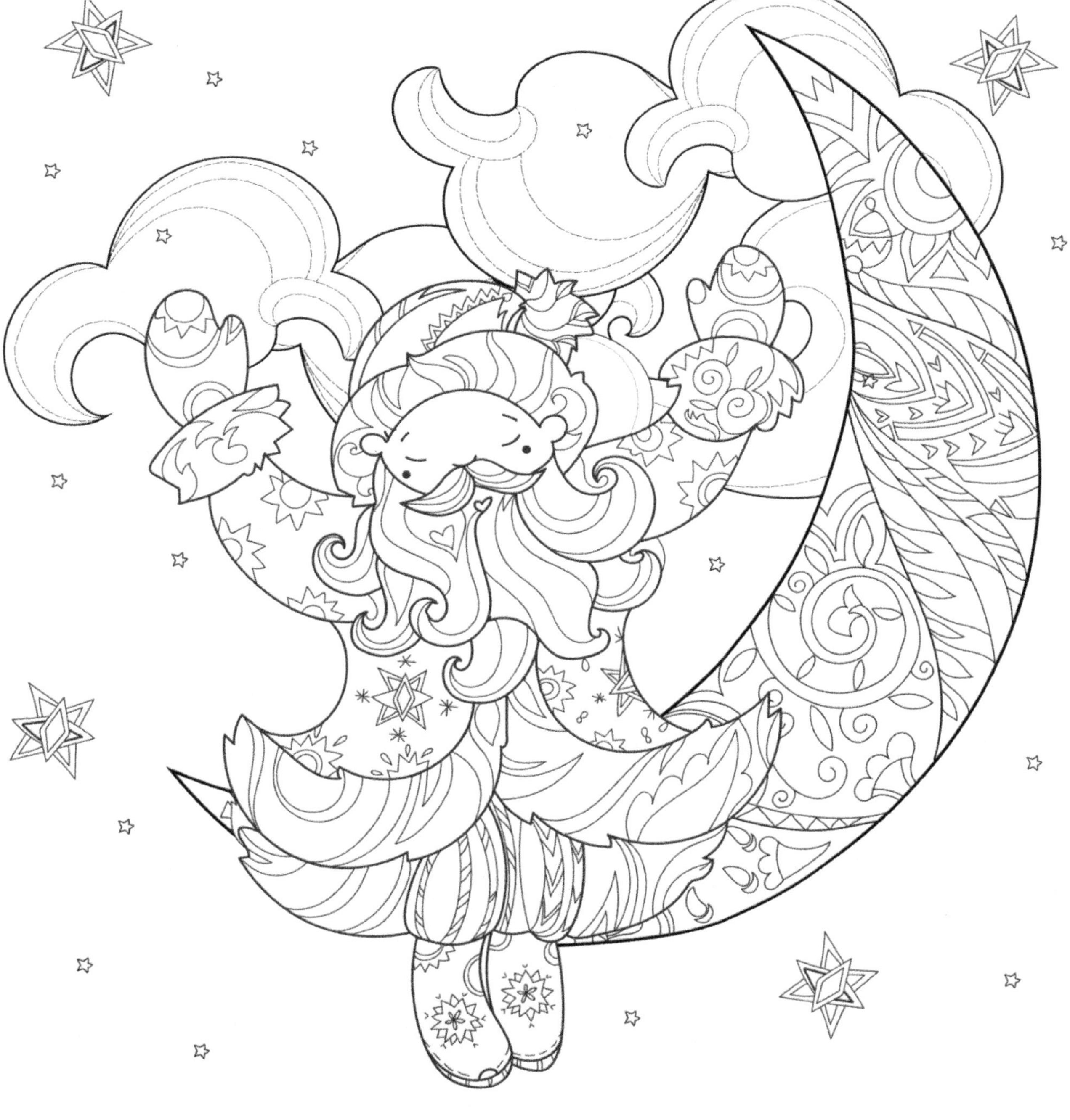

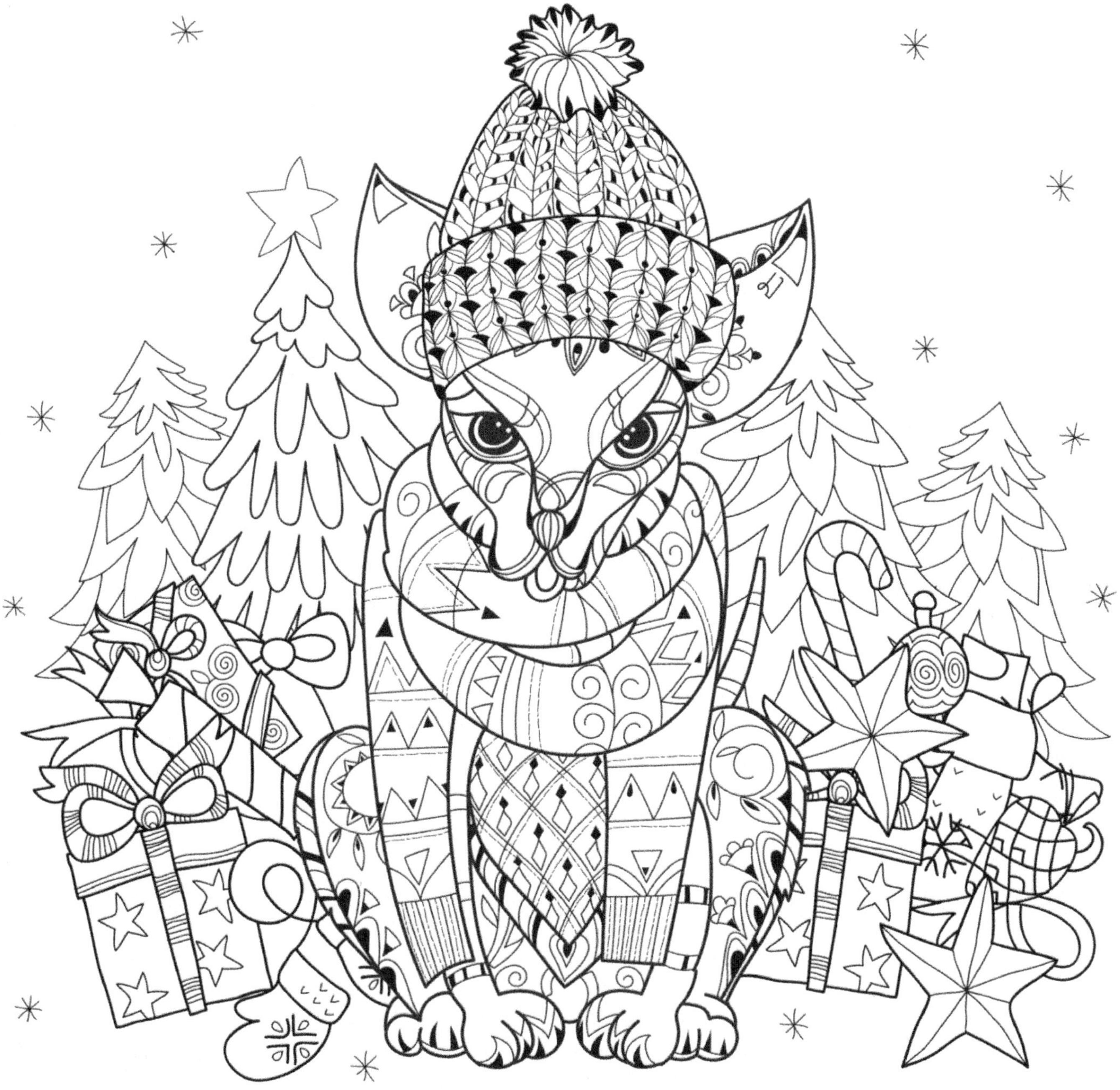

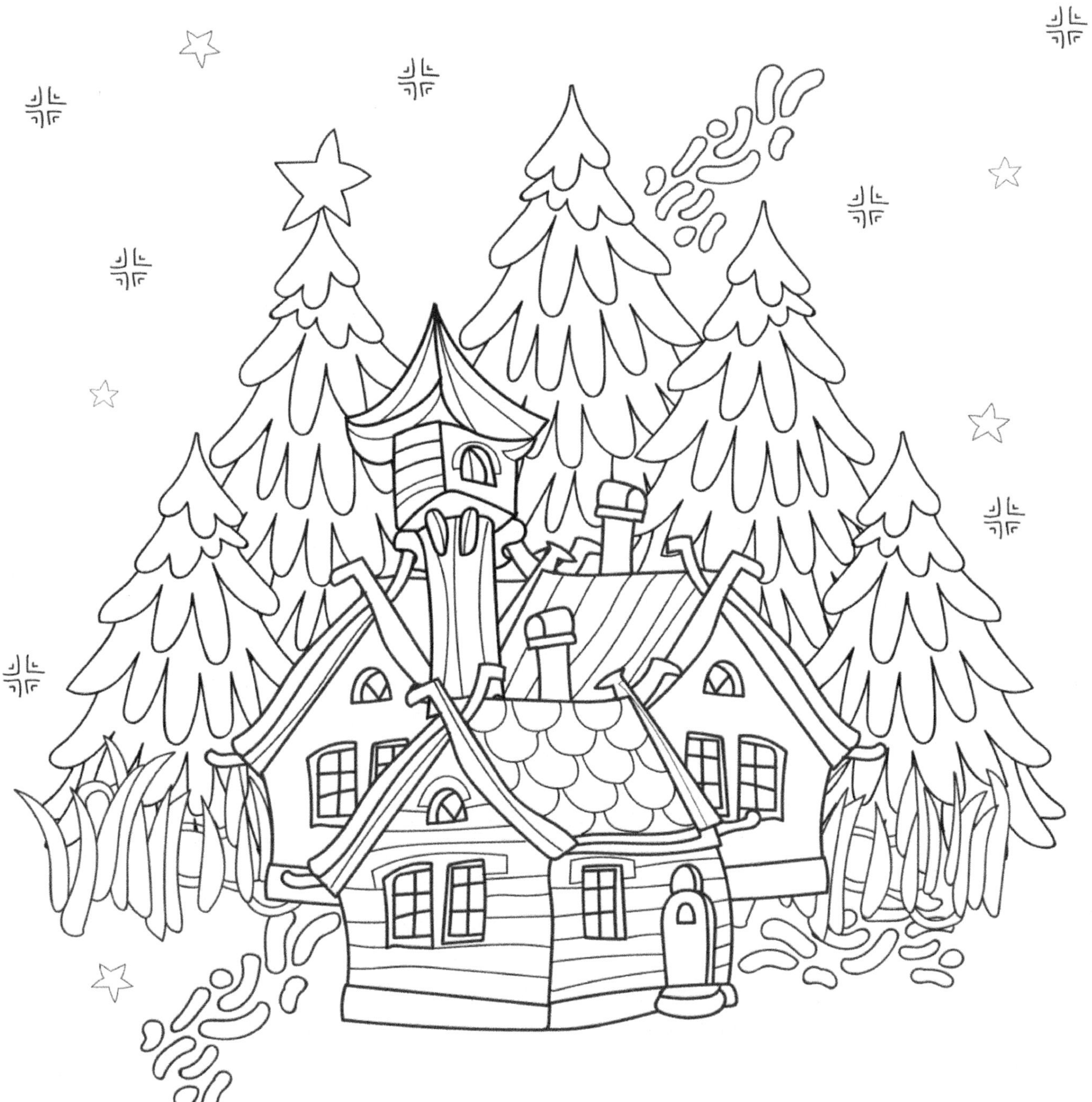

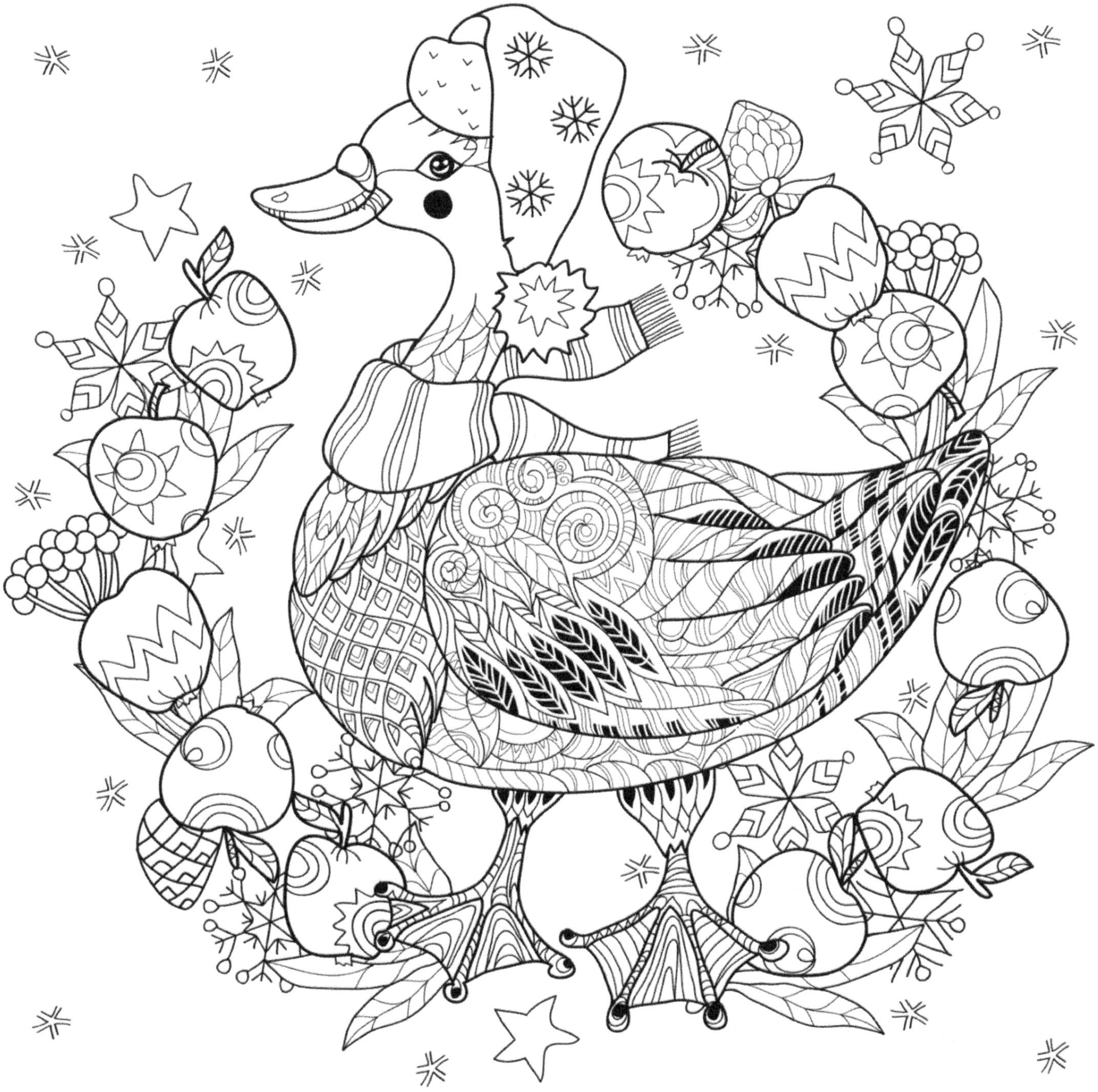

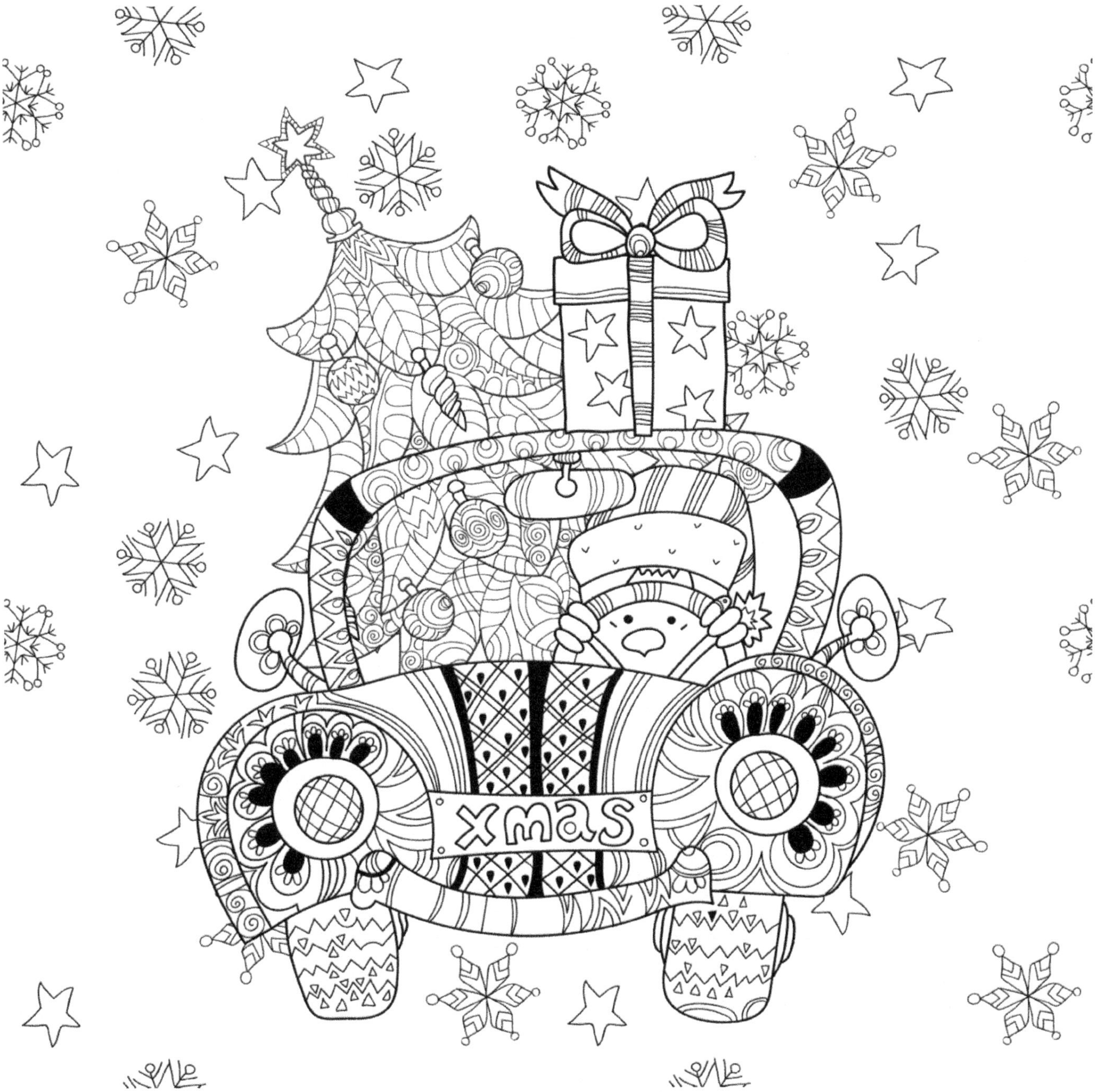
xmas

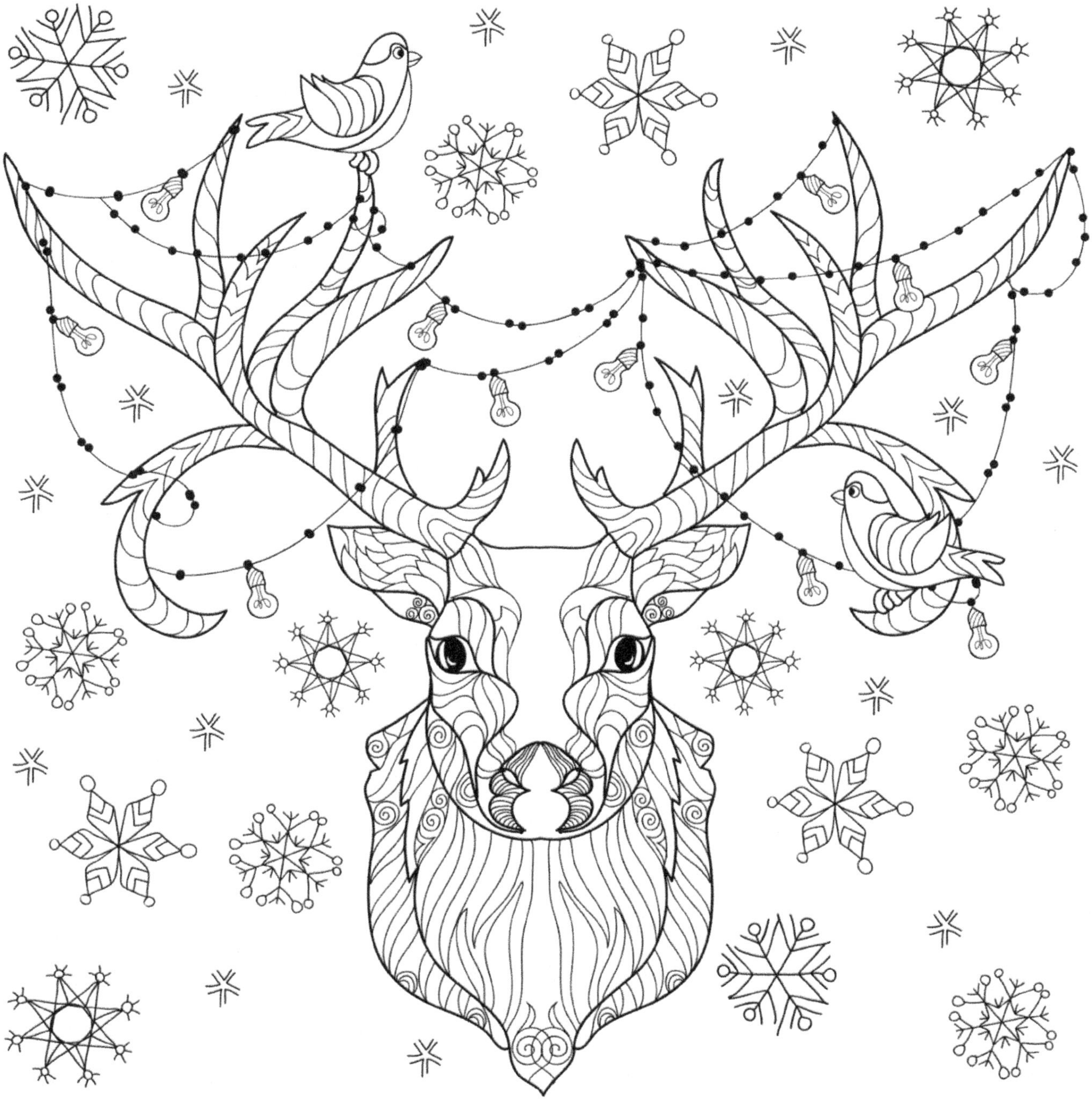

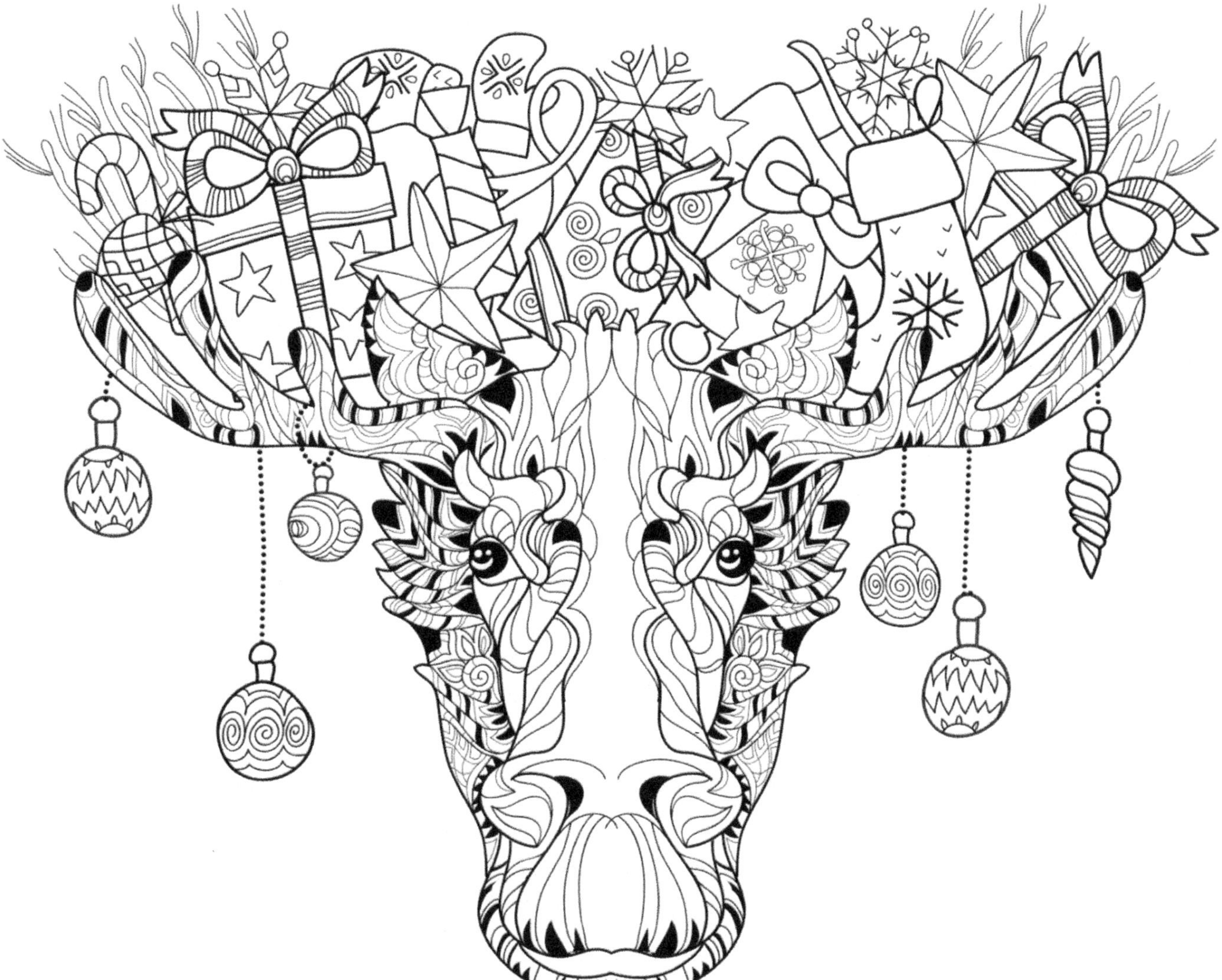

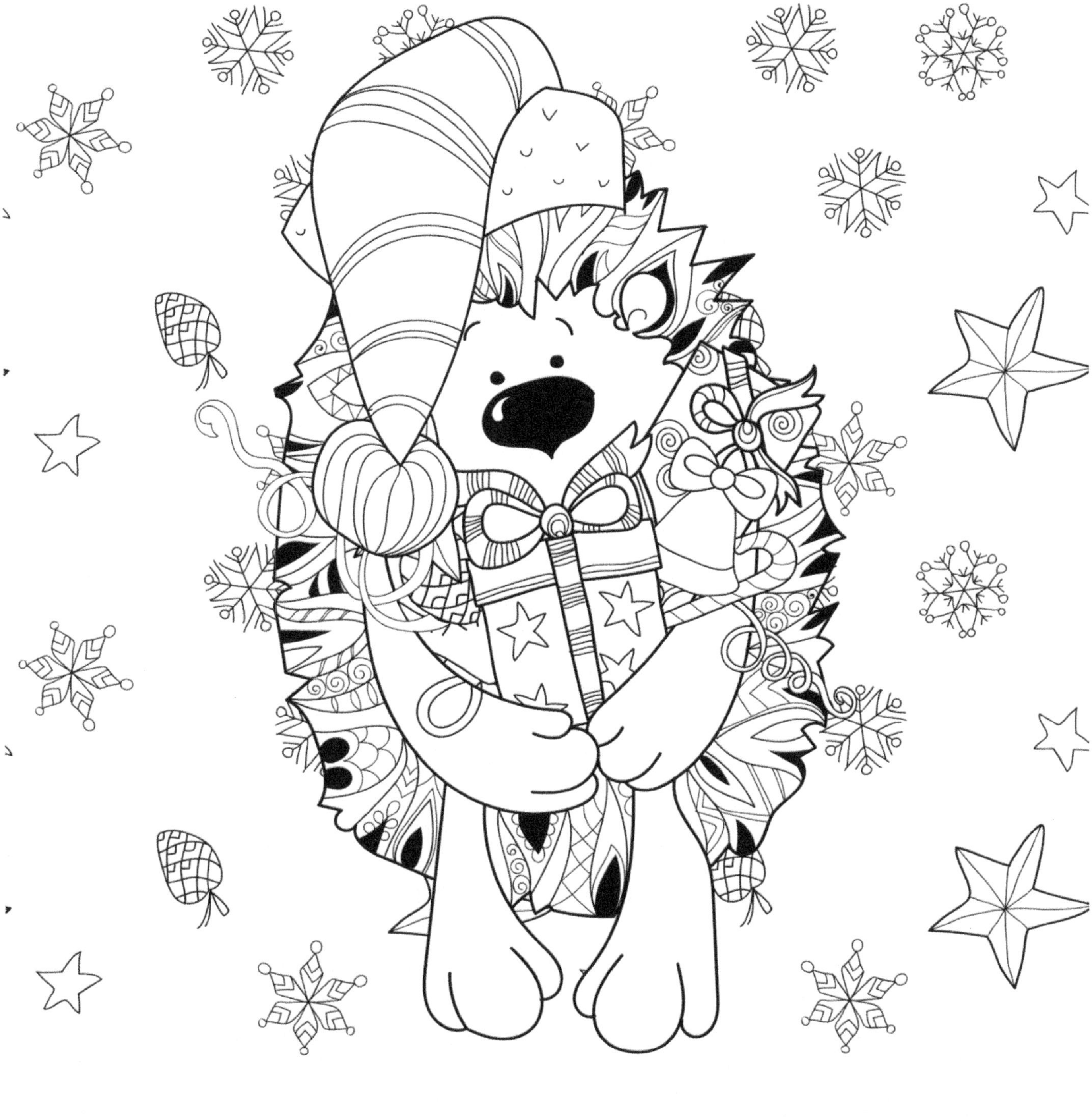

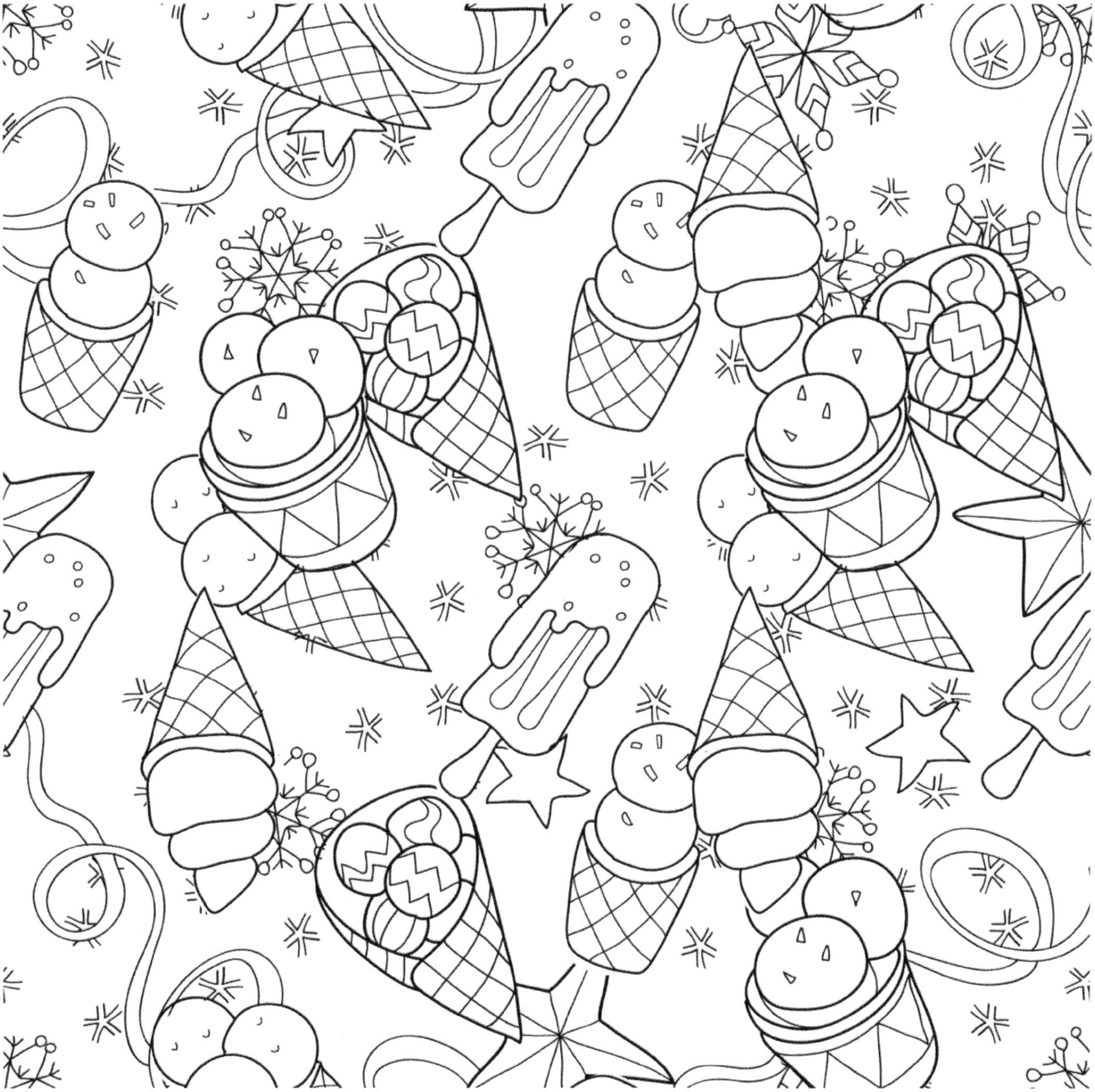

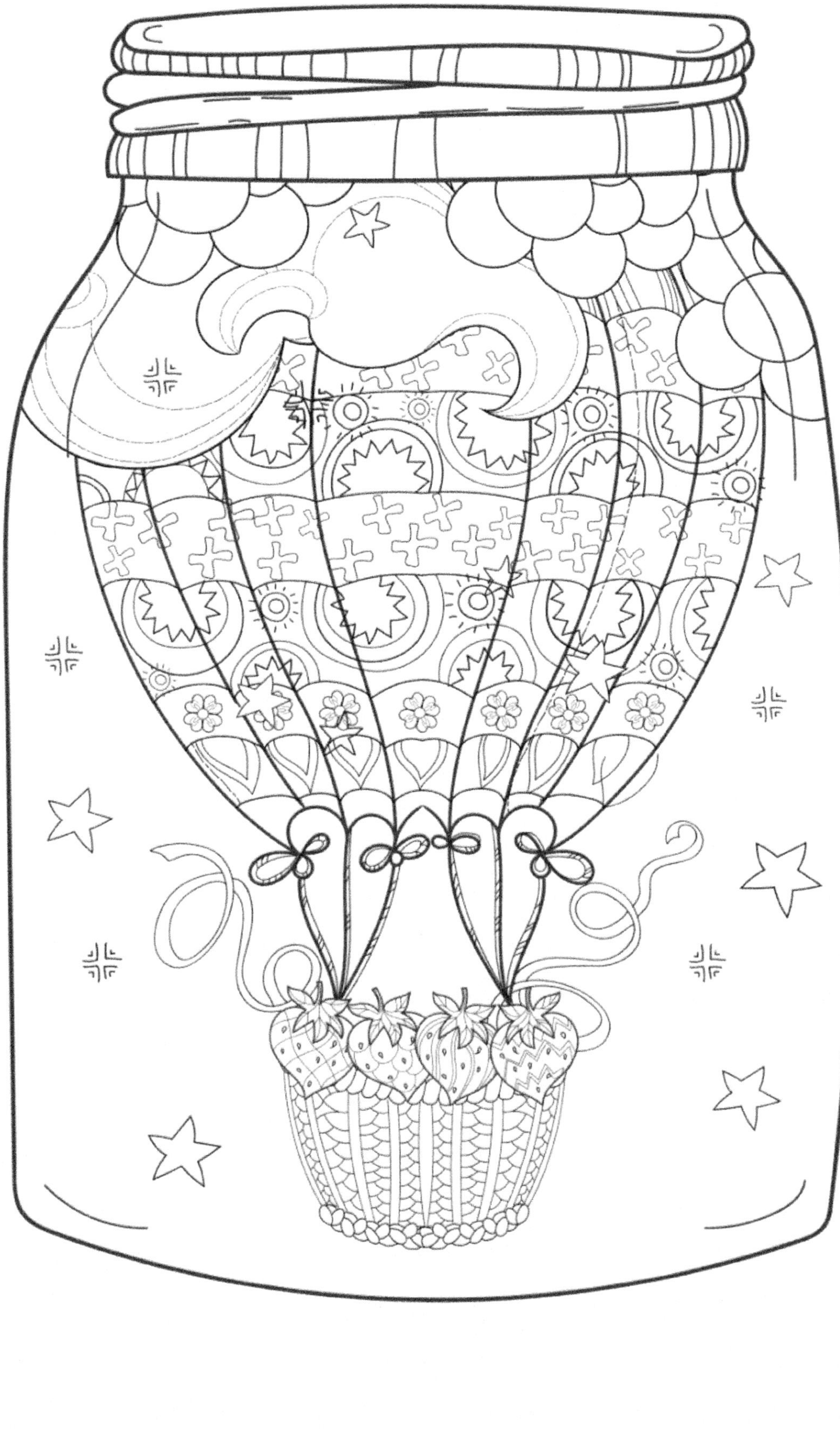

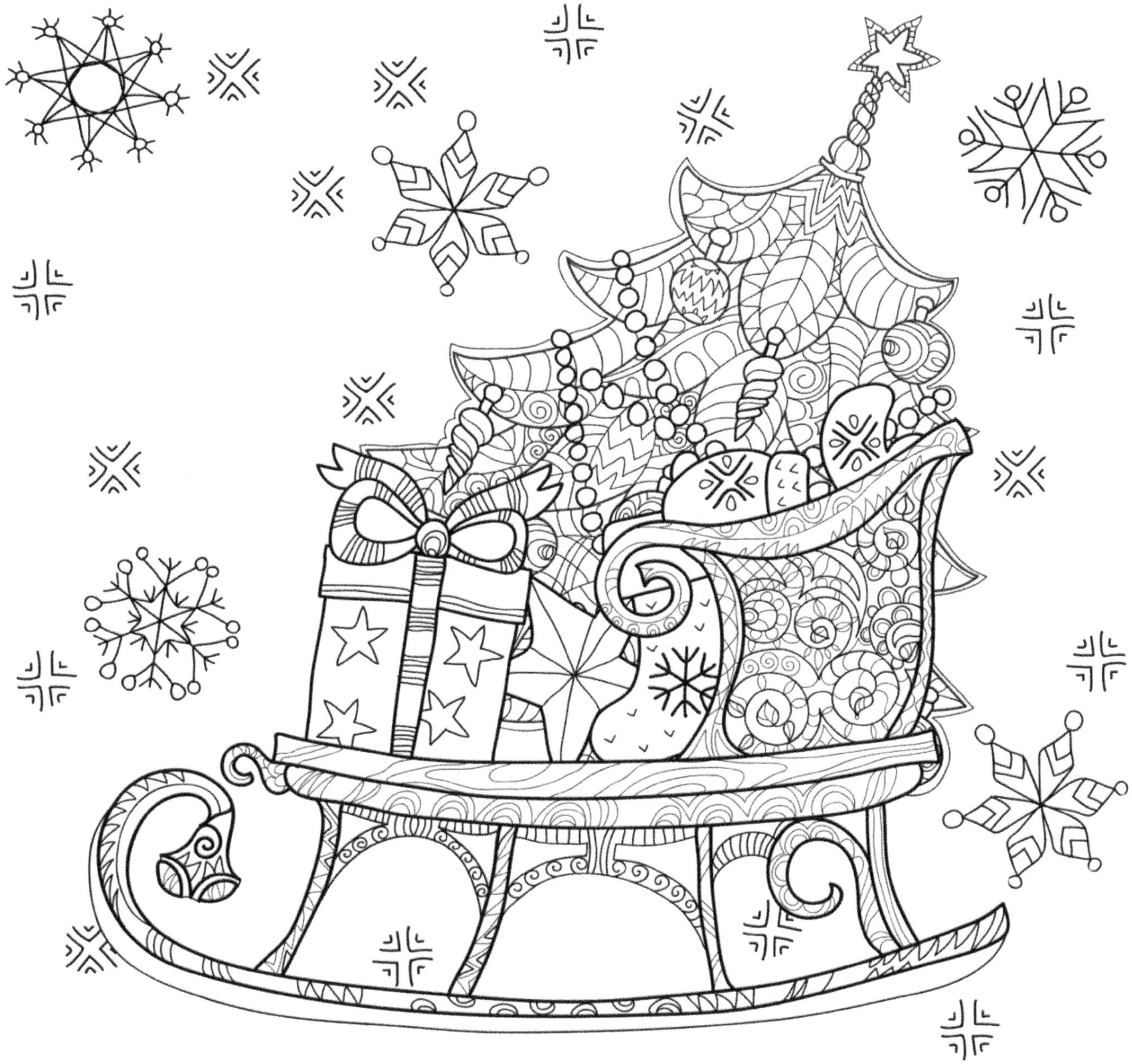

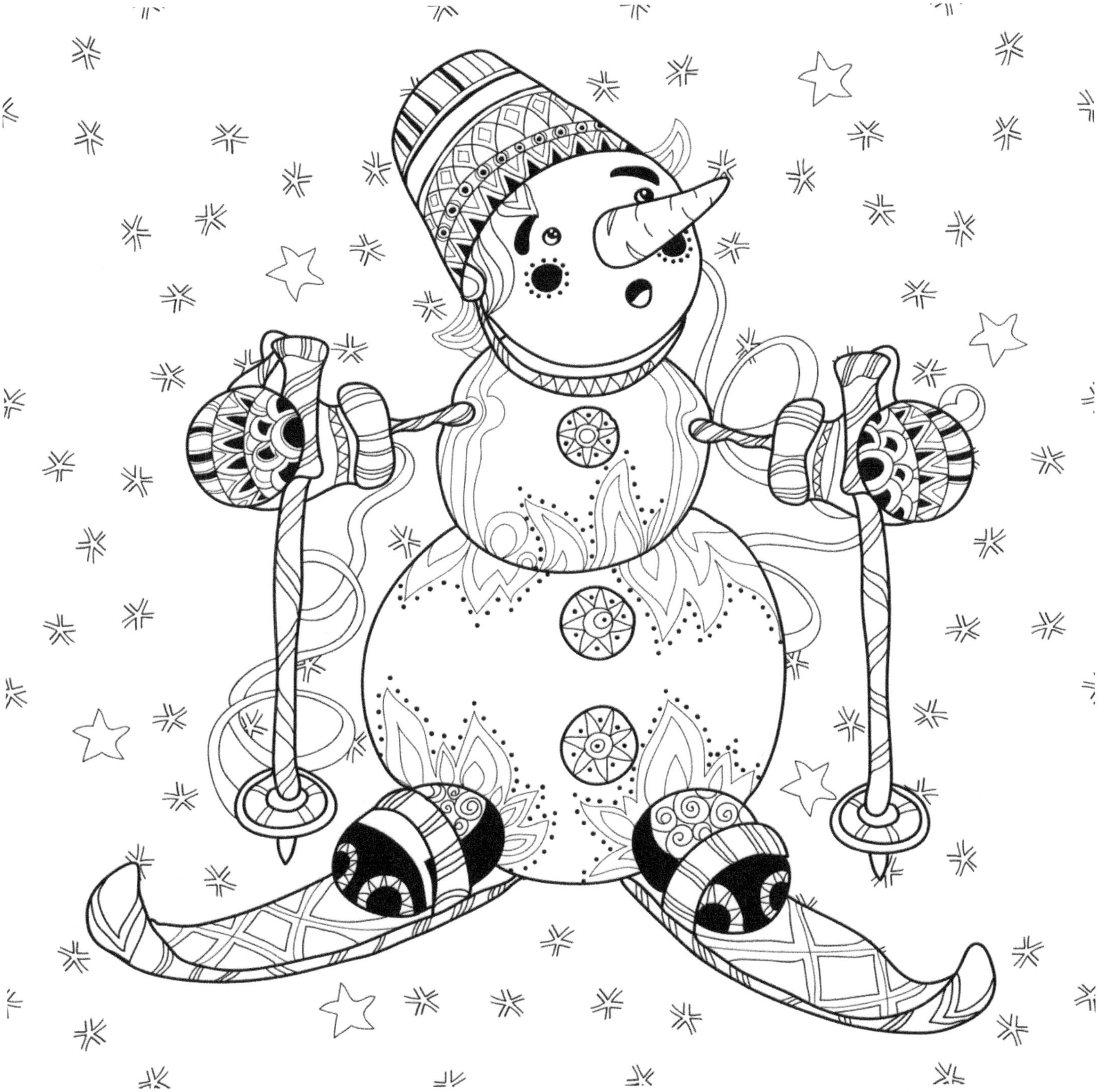

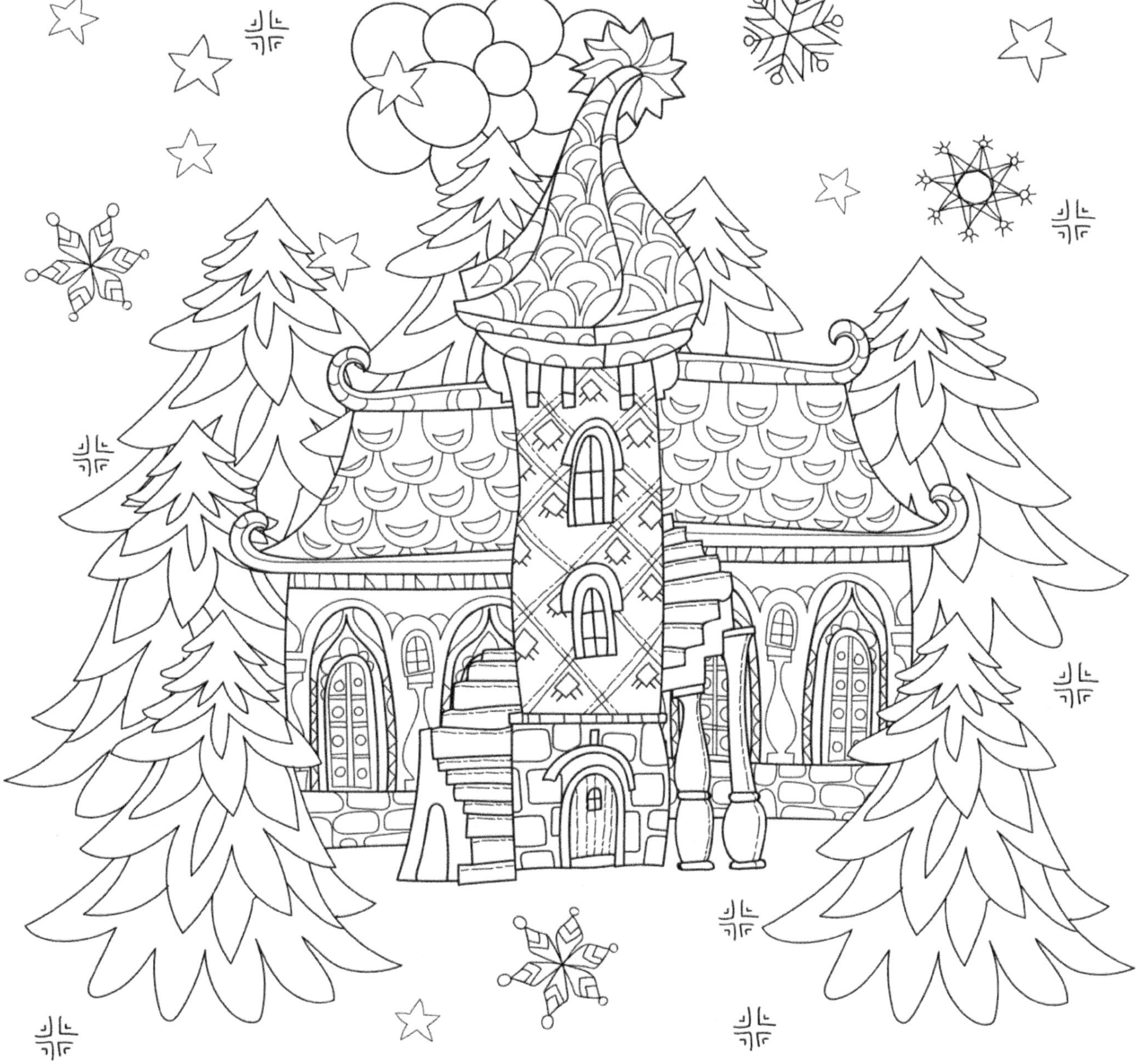

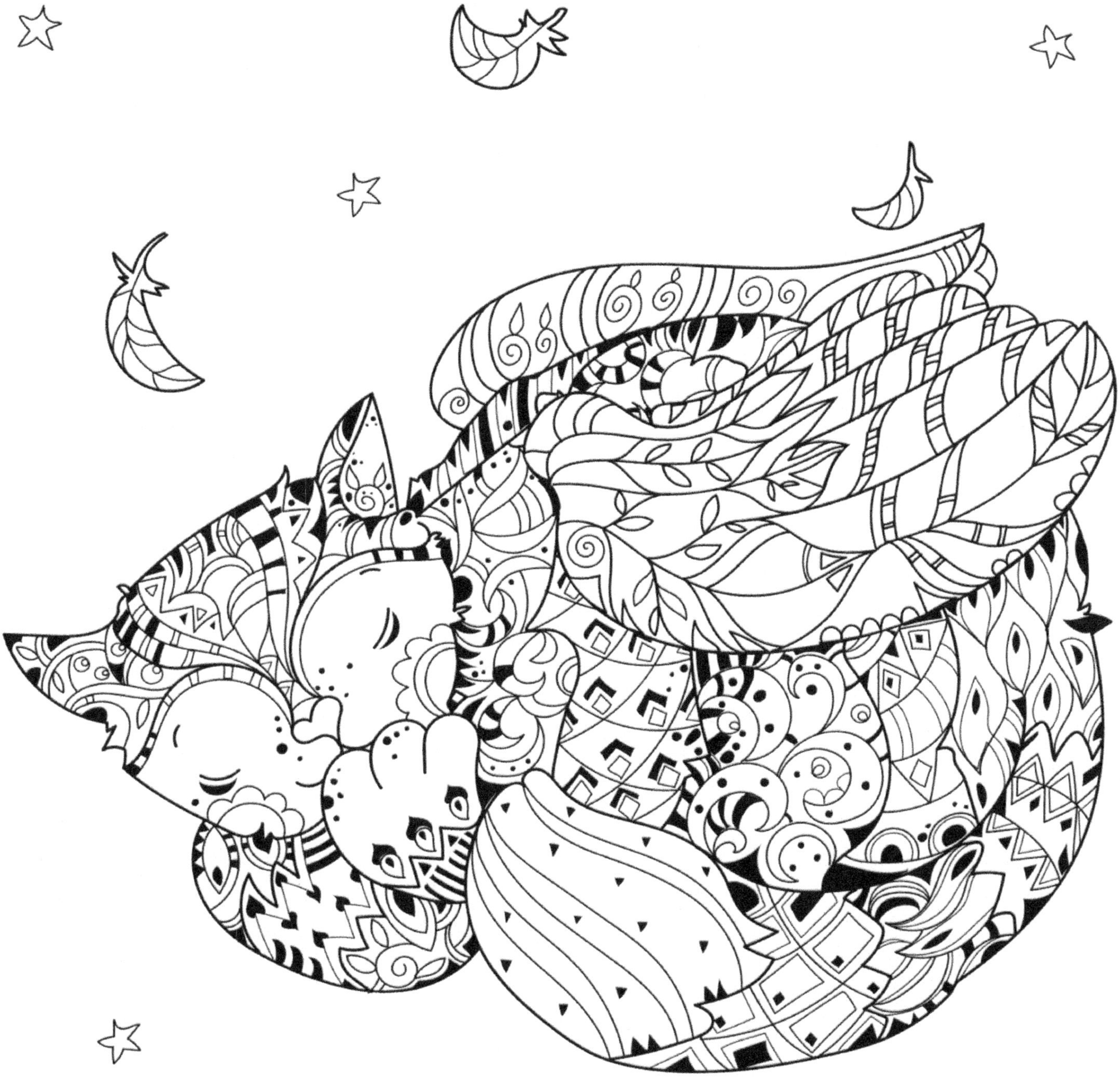

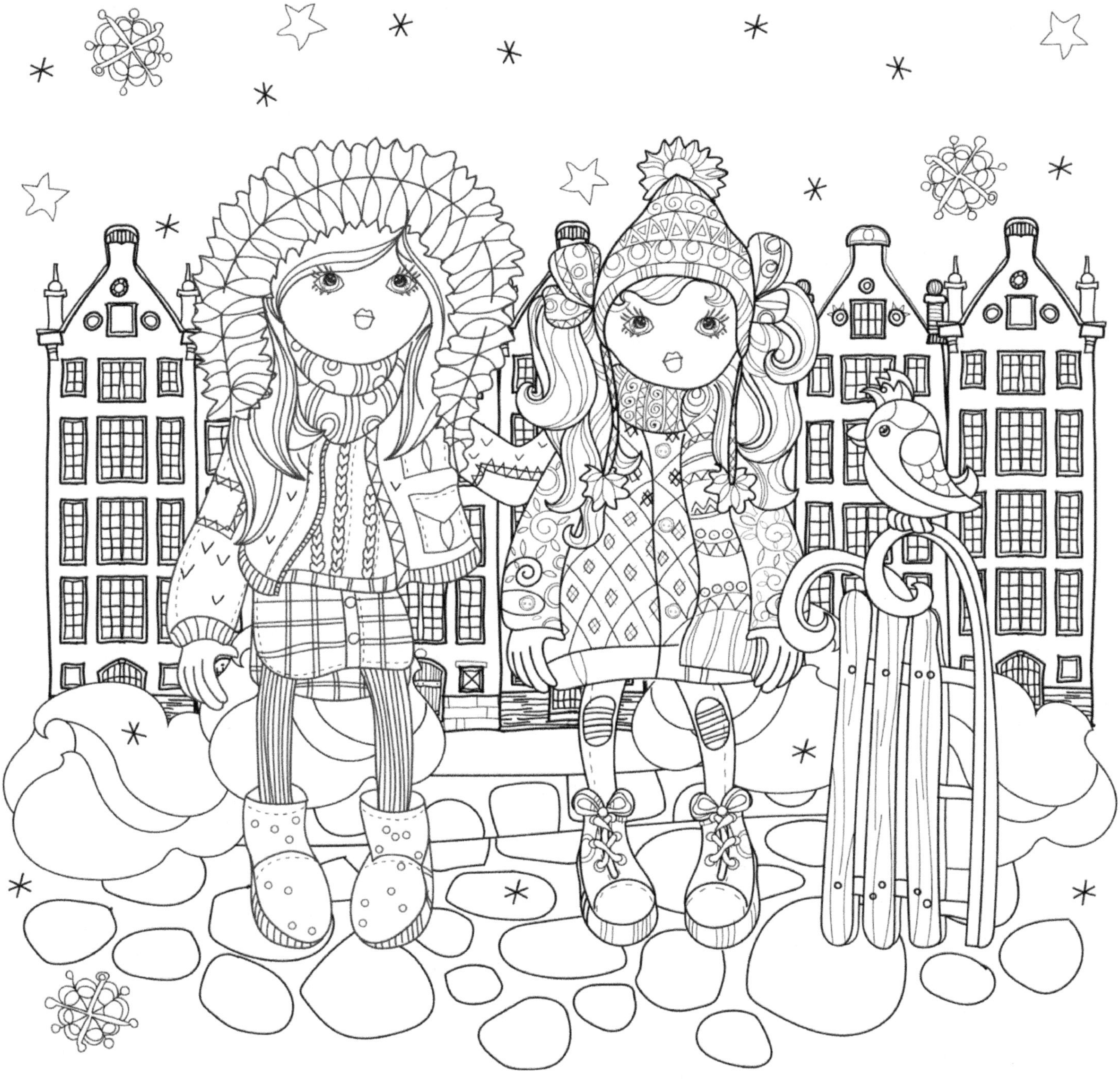

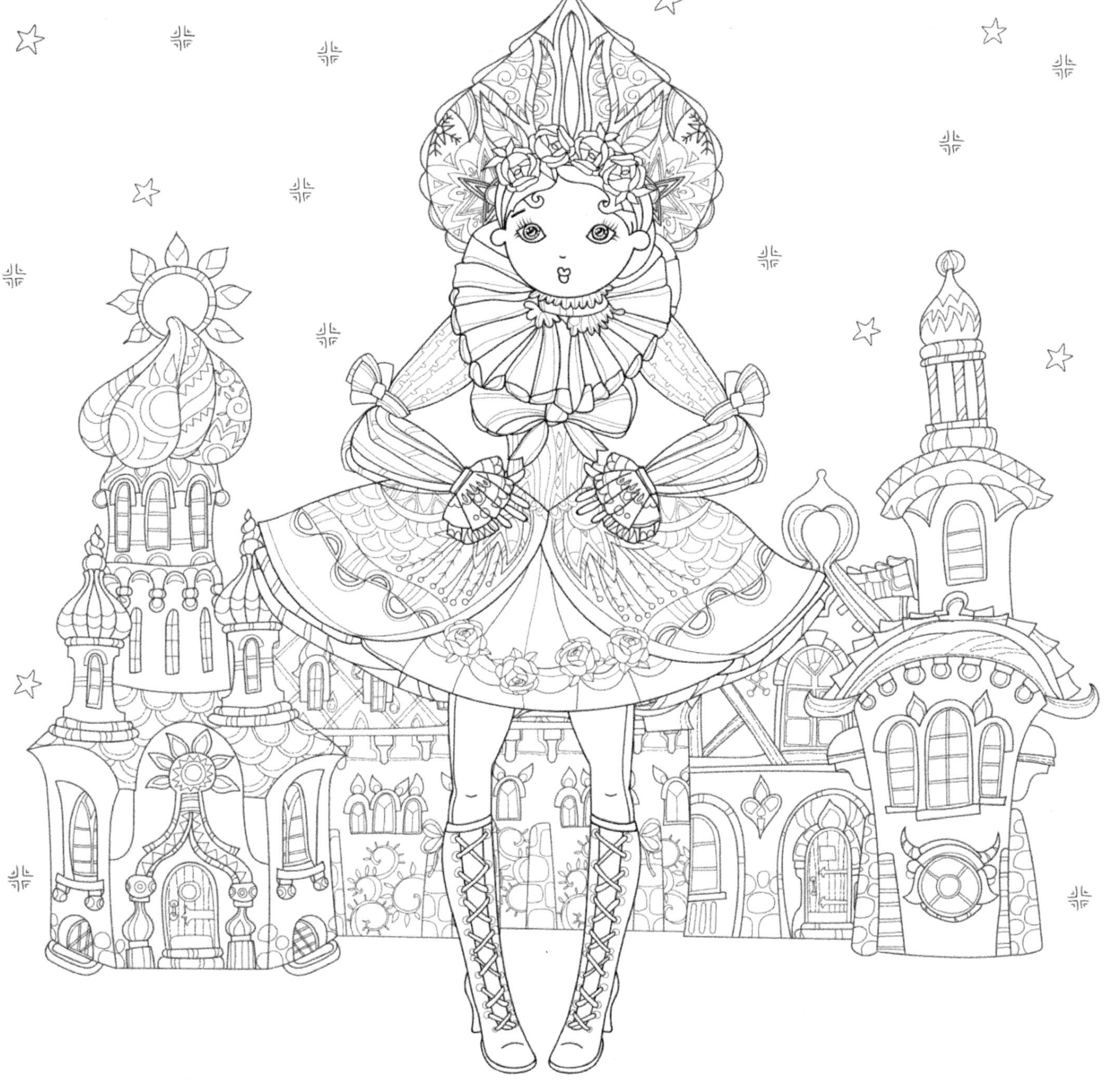

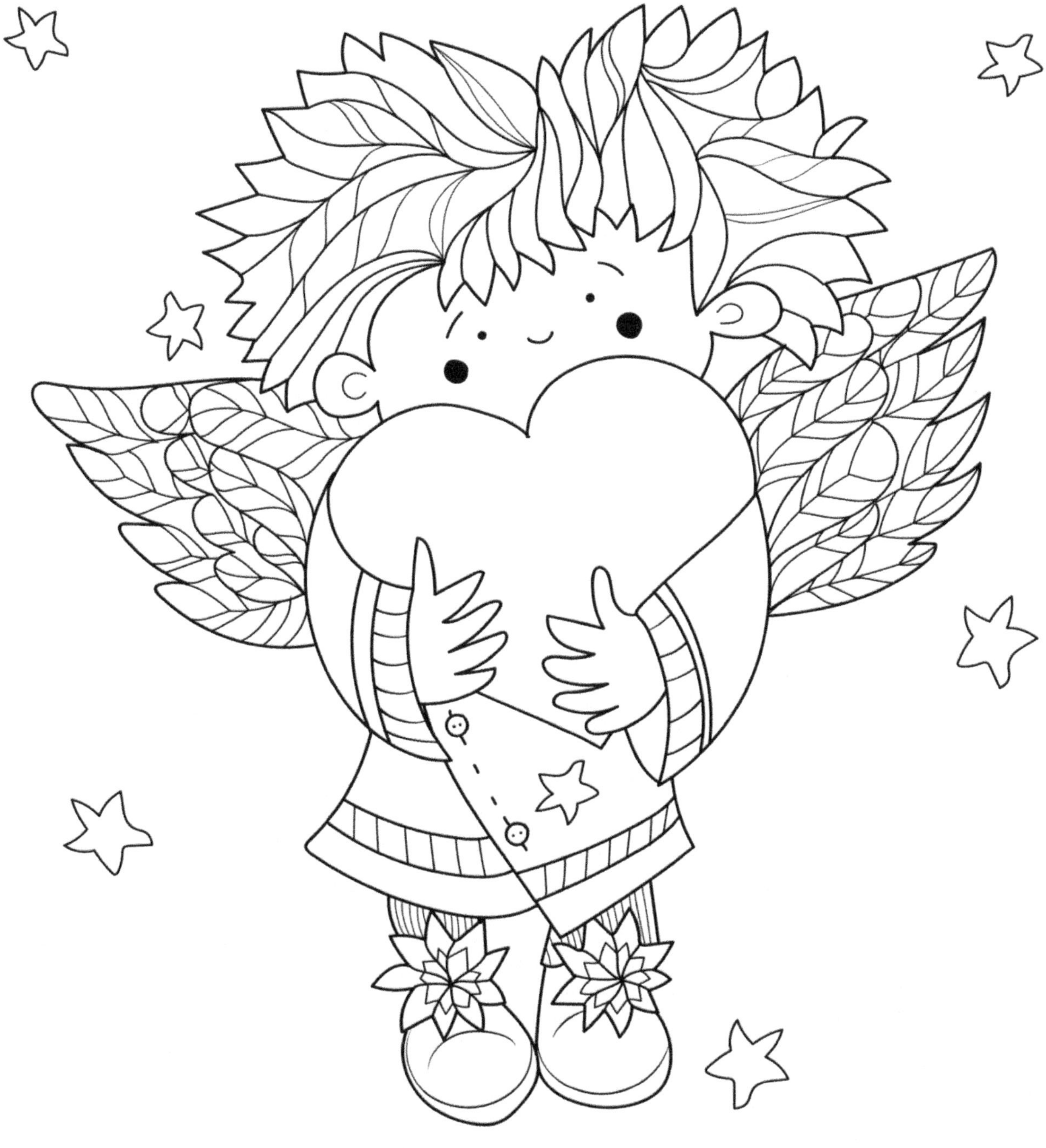

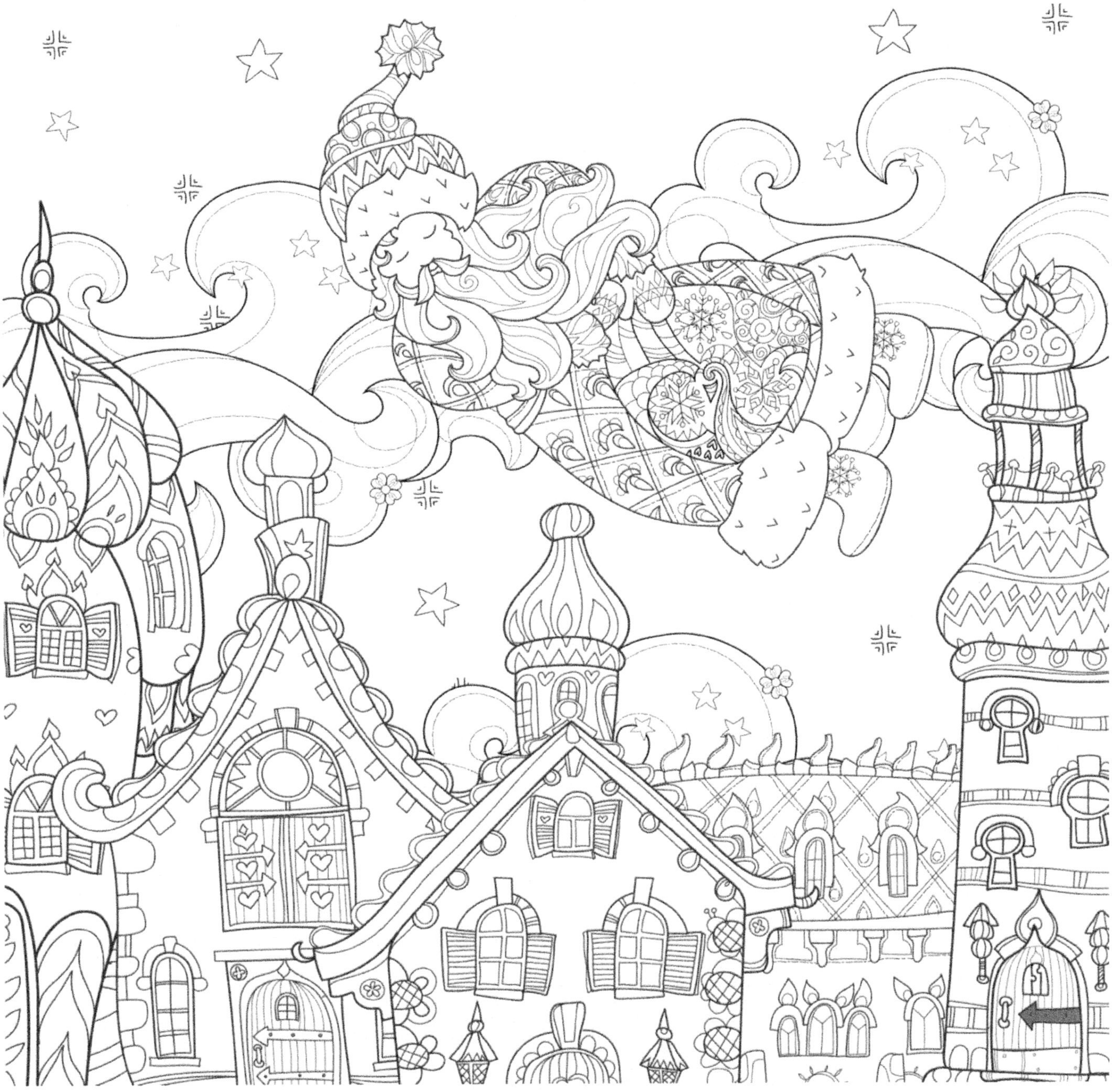

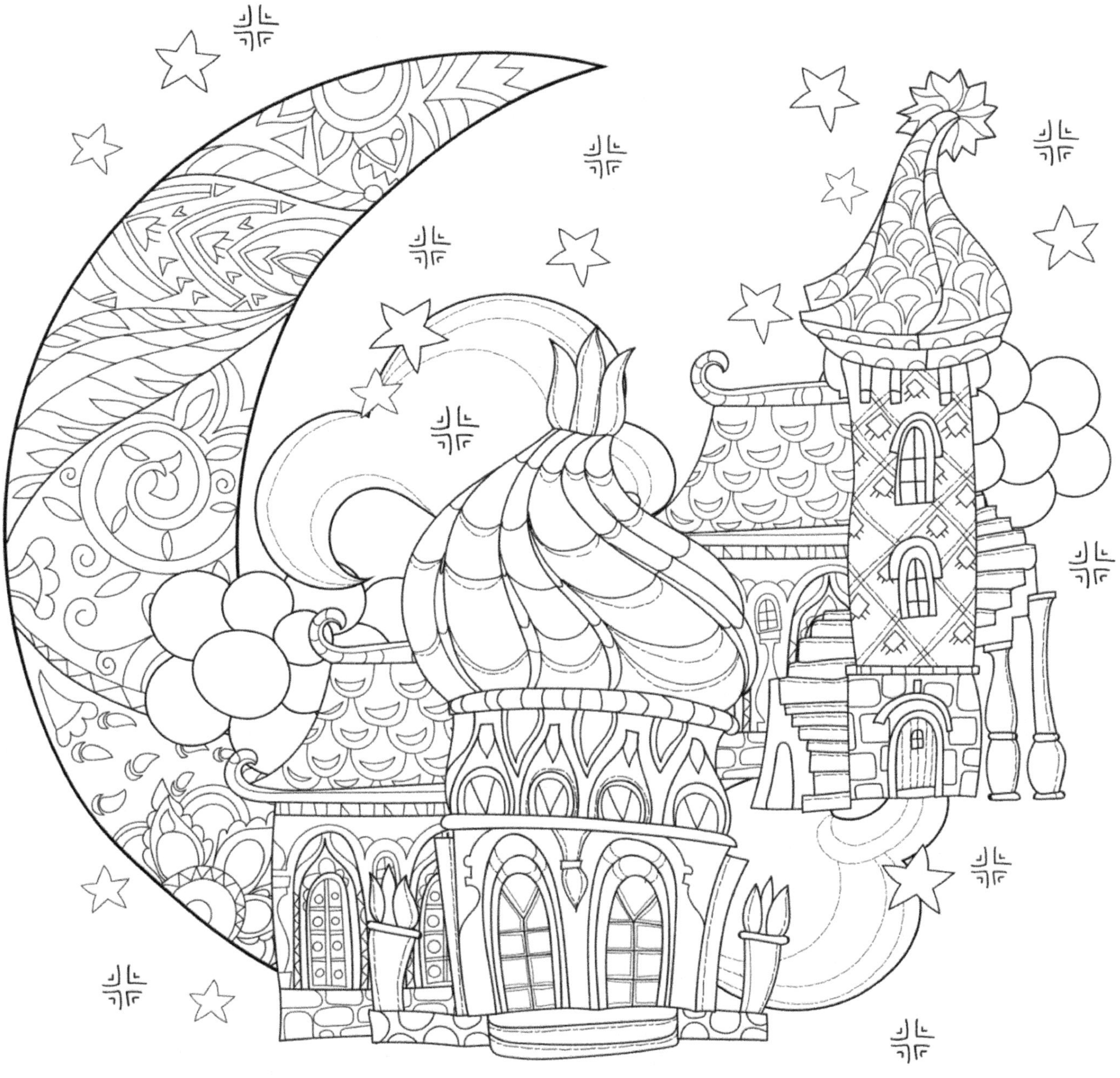

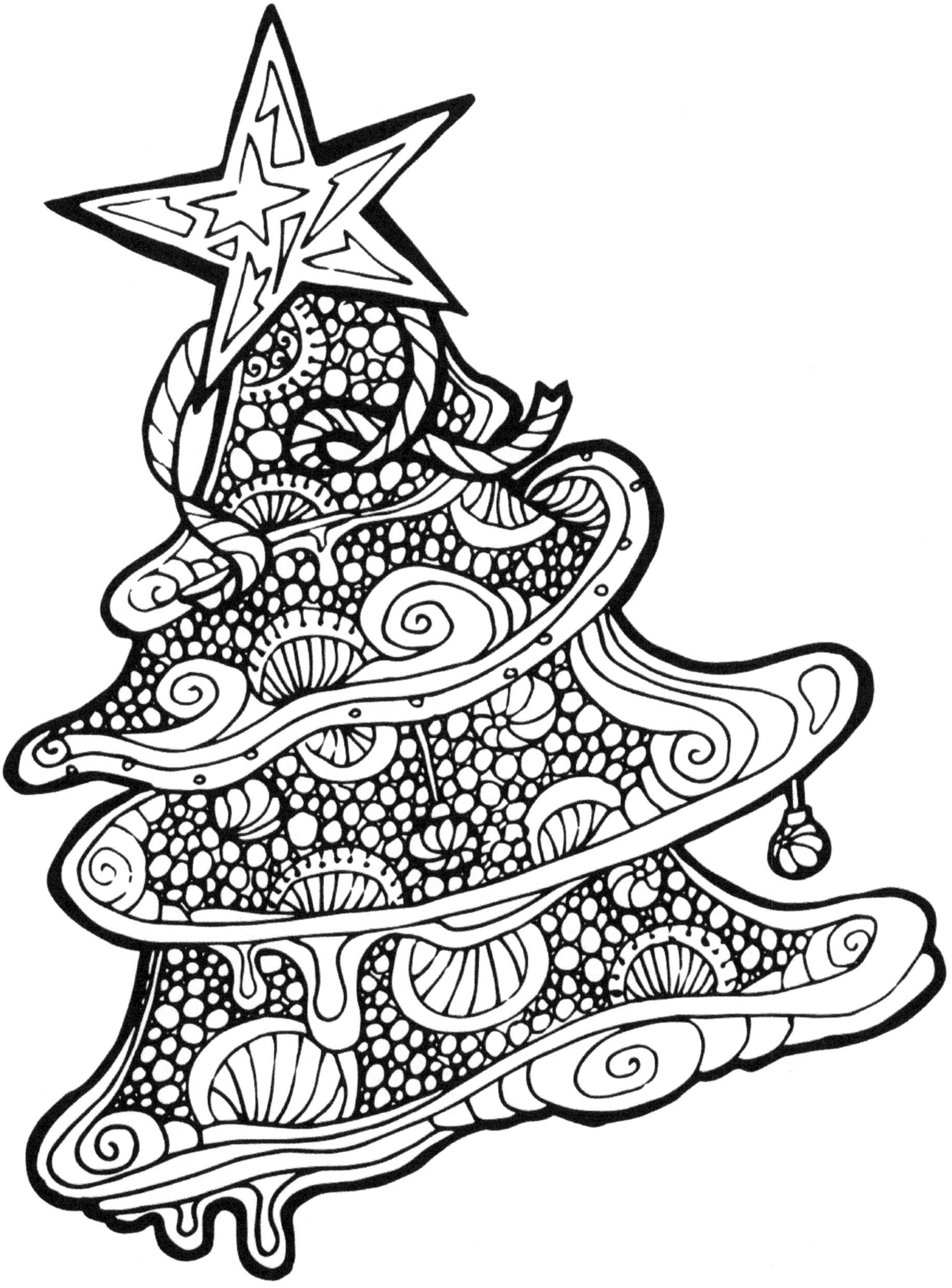

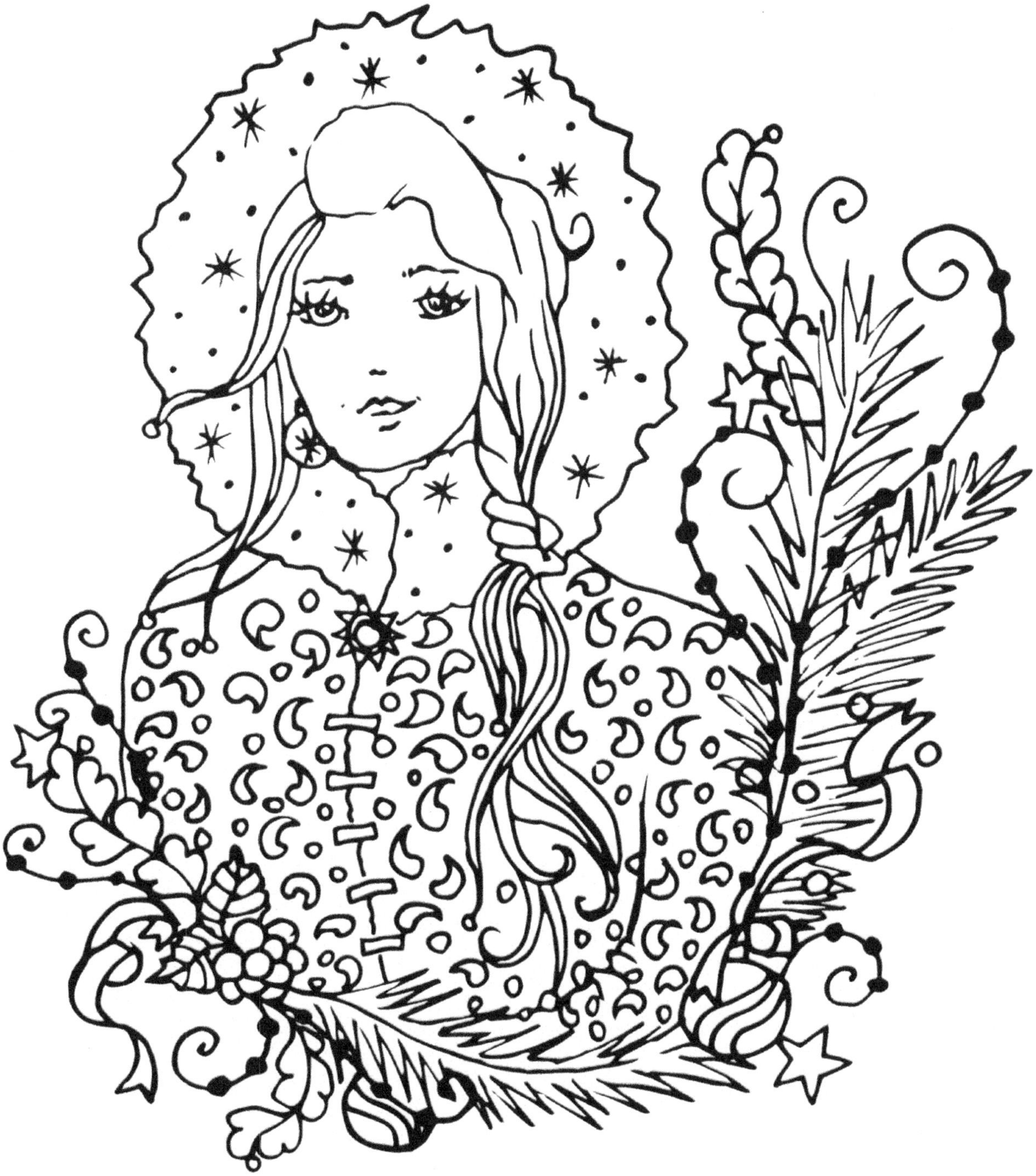

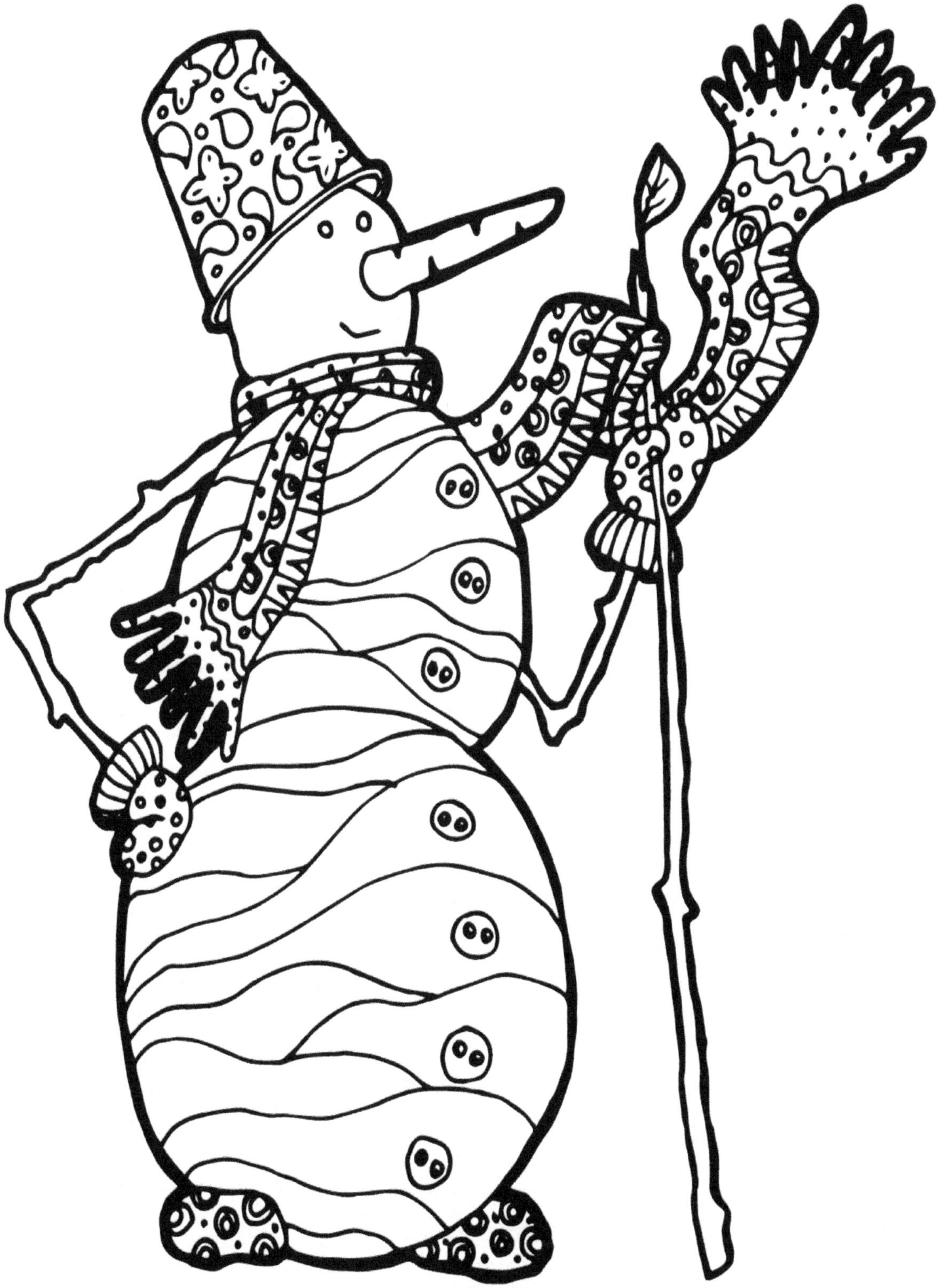

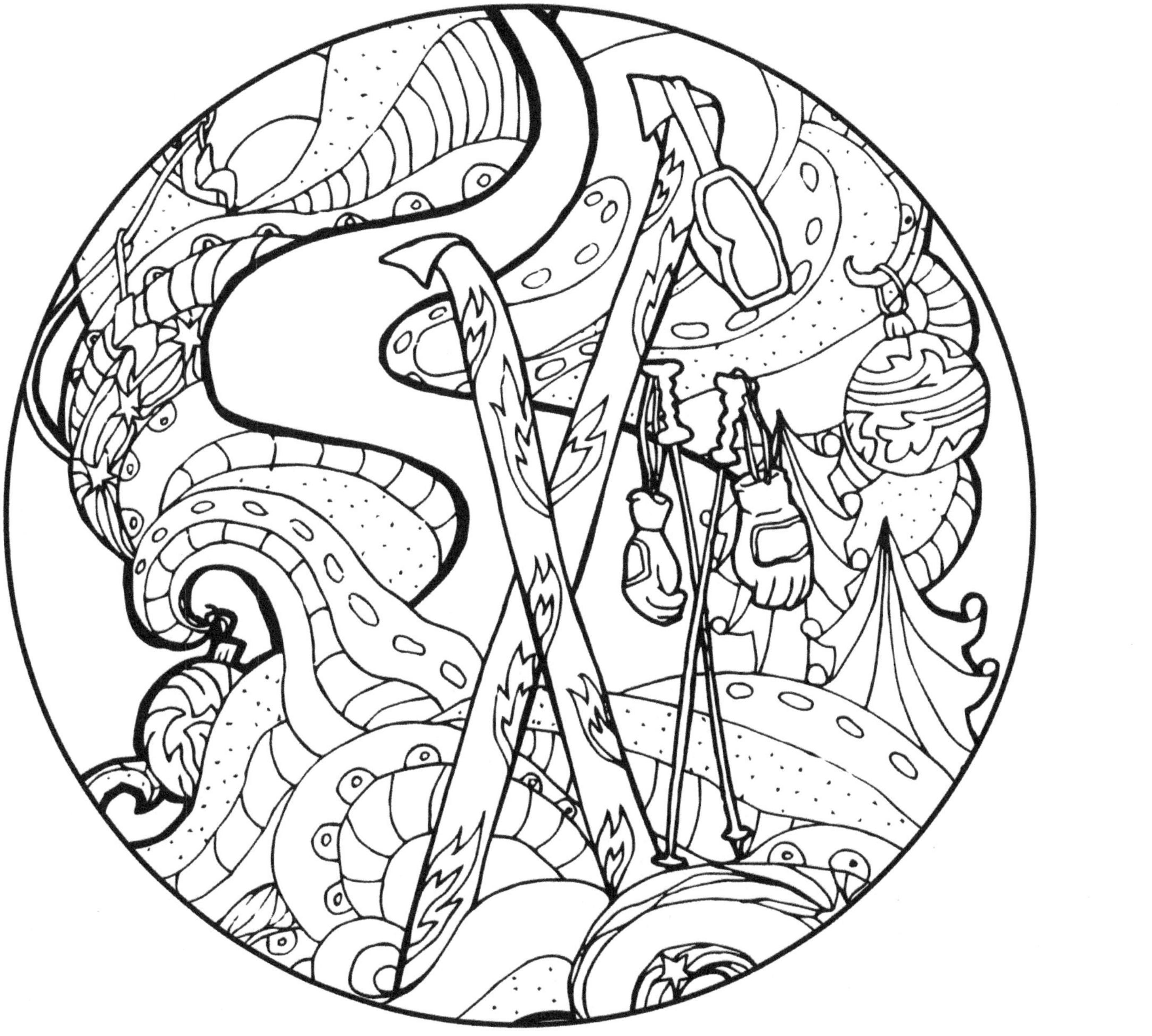

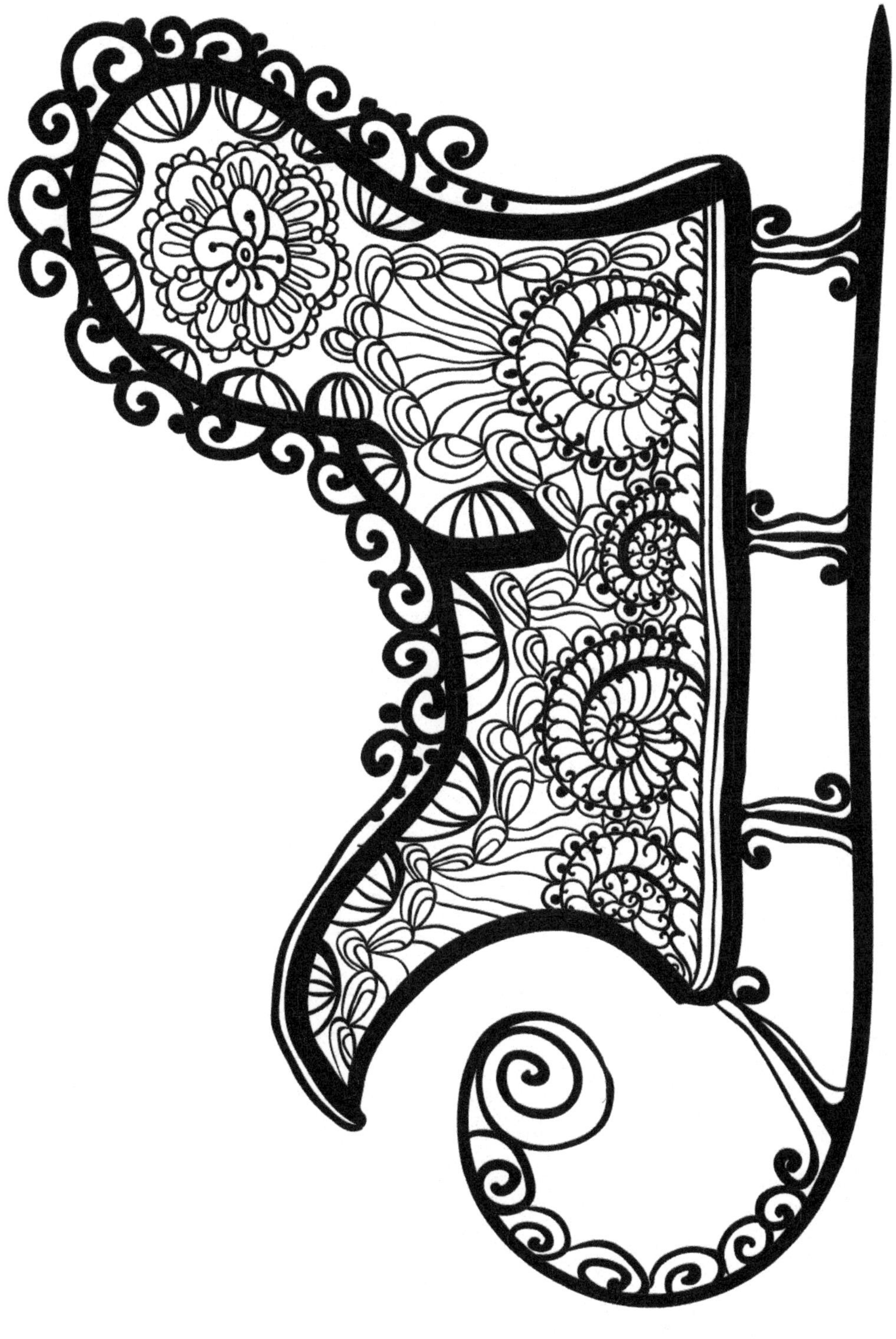

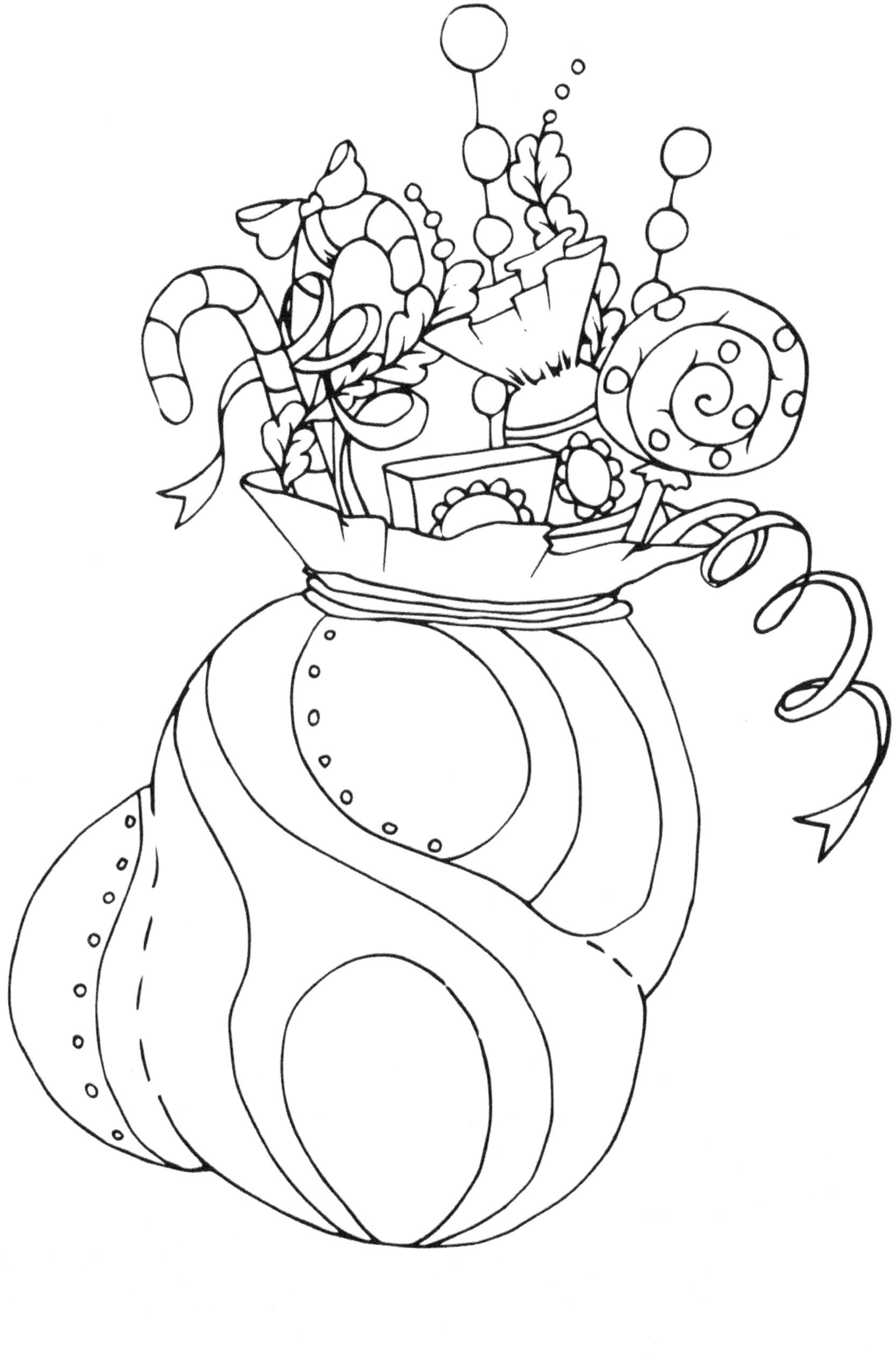

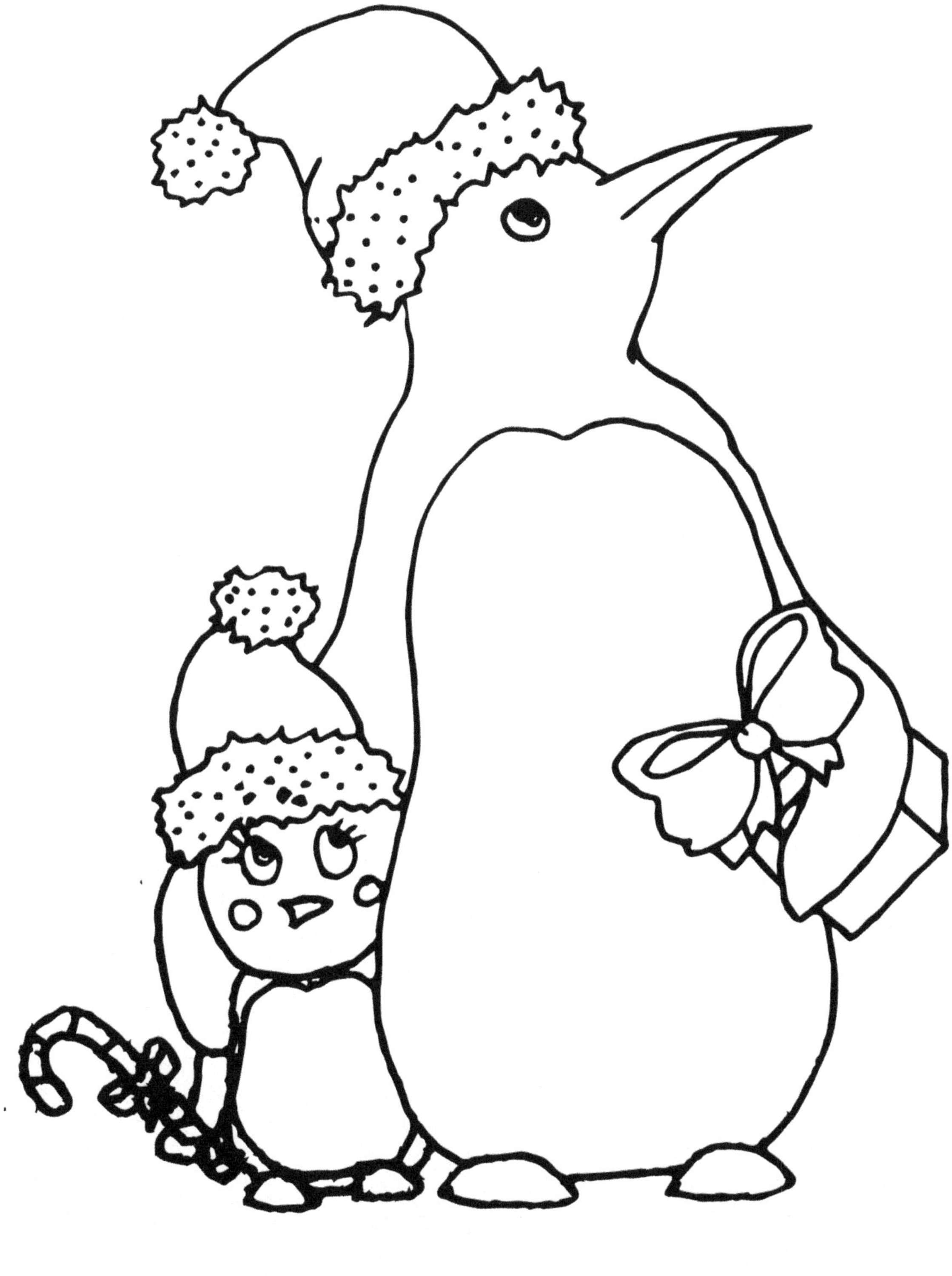

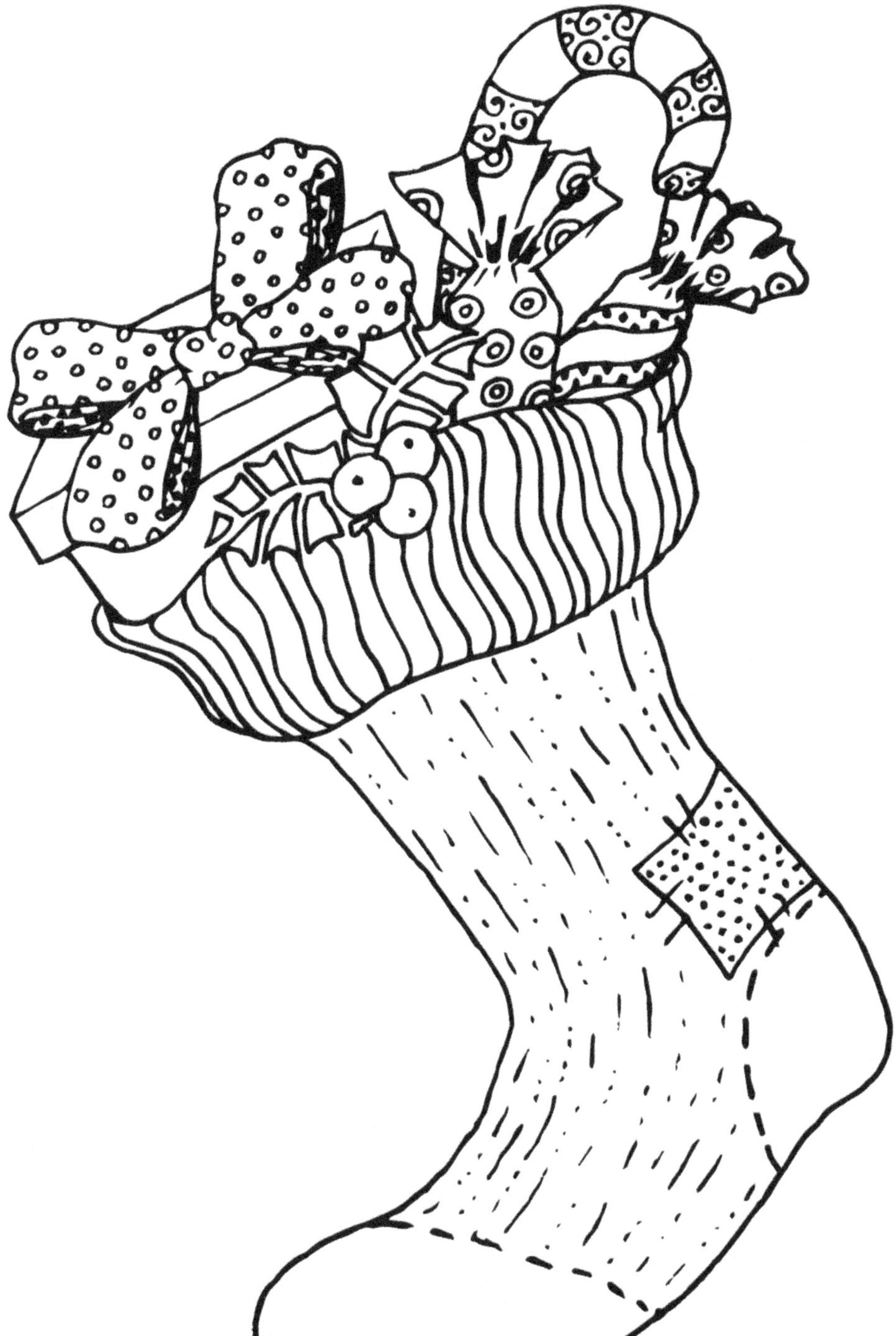

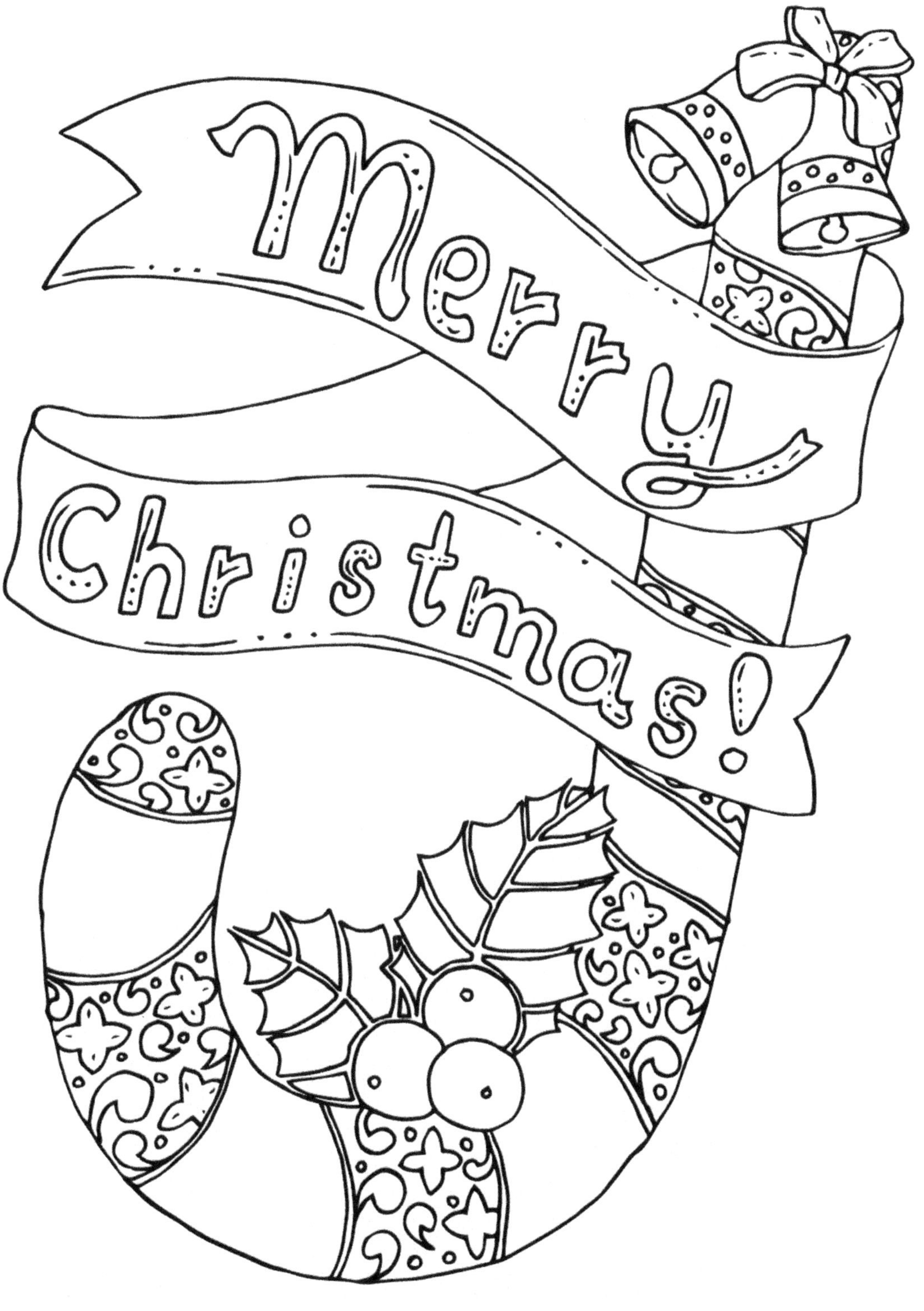
Merry
Christmas!

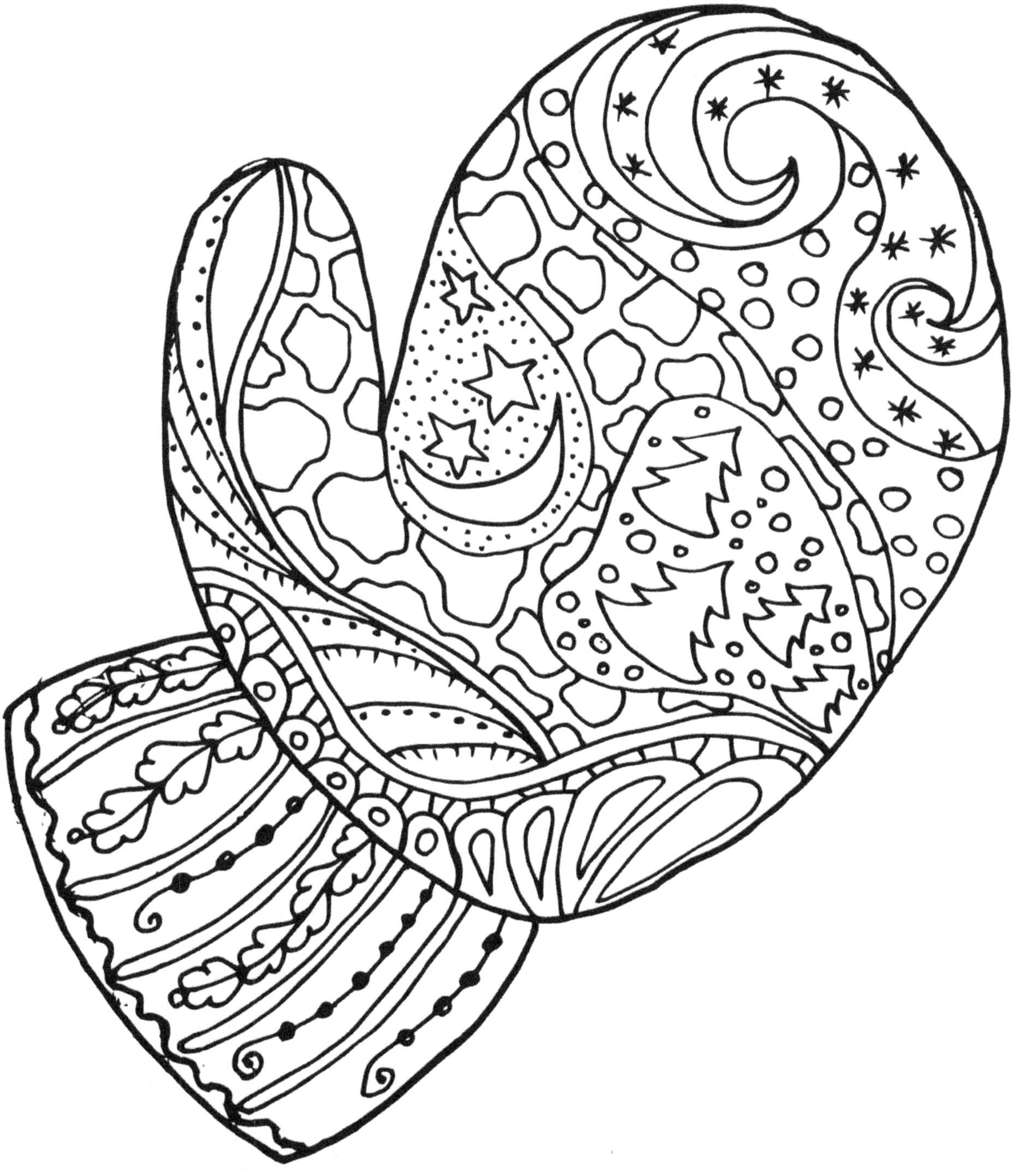

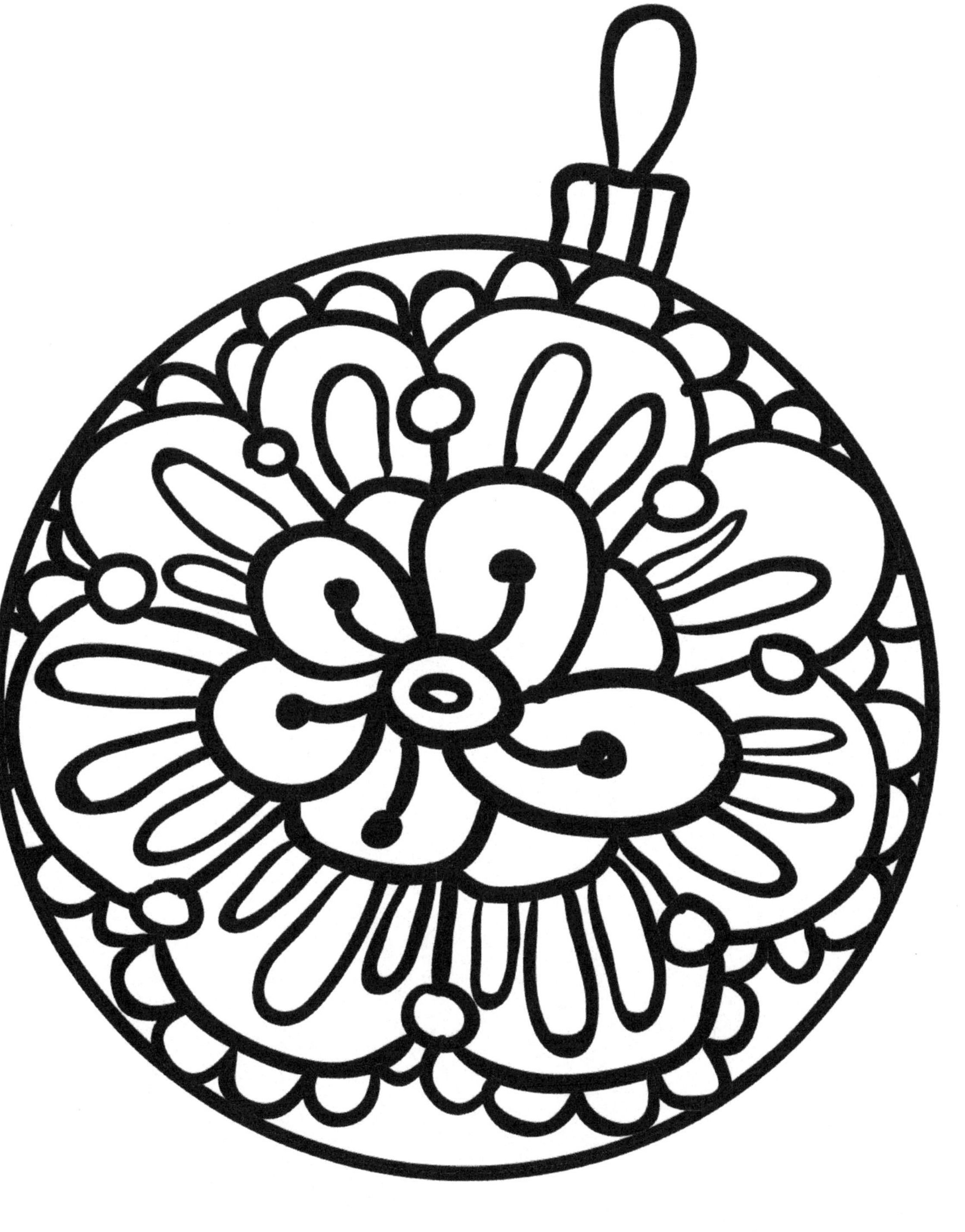

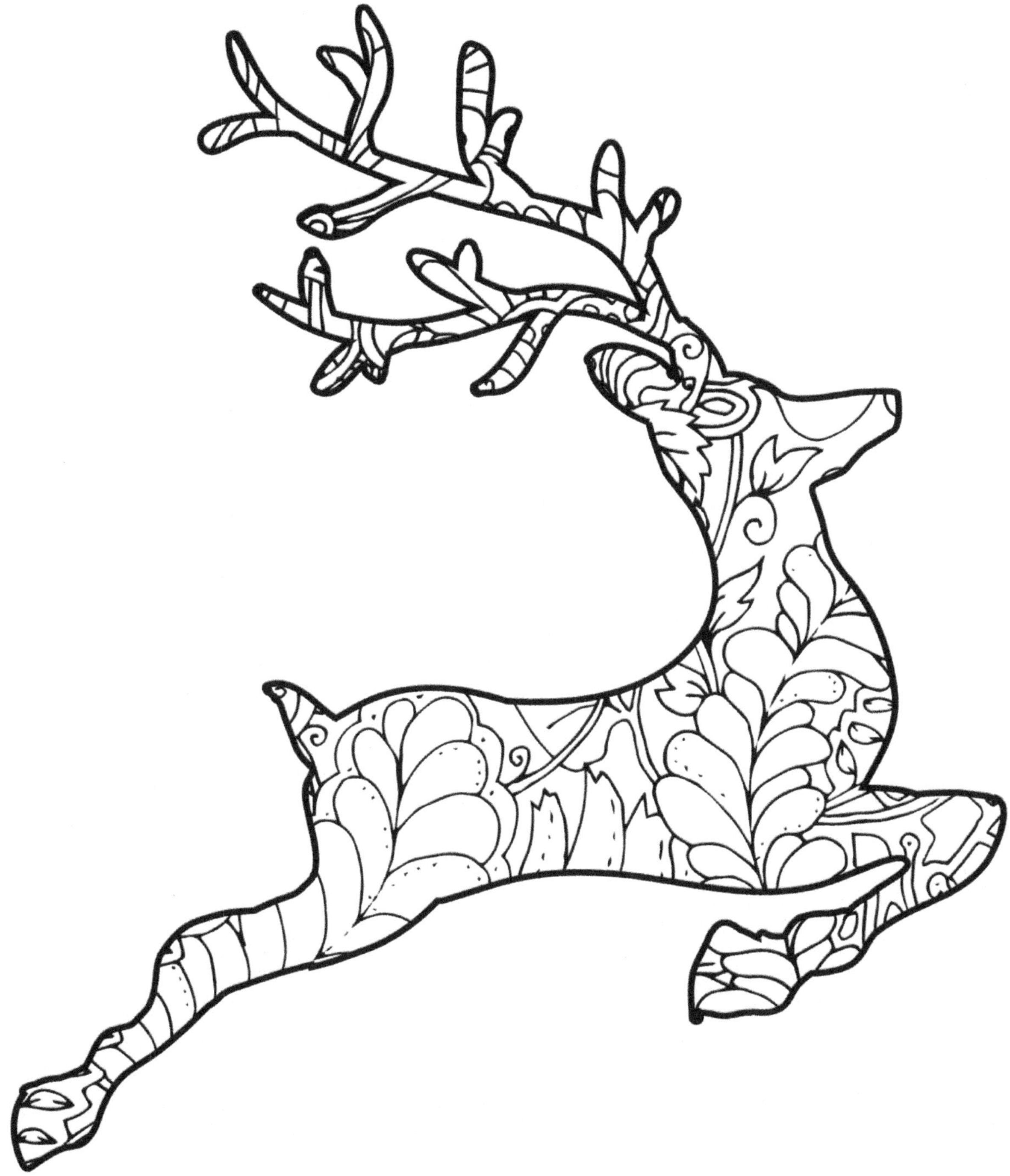

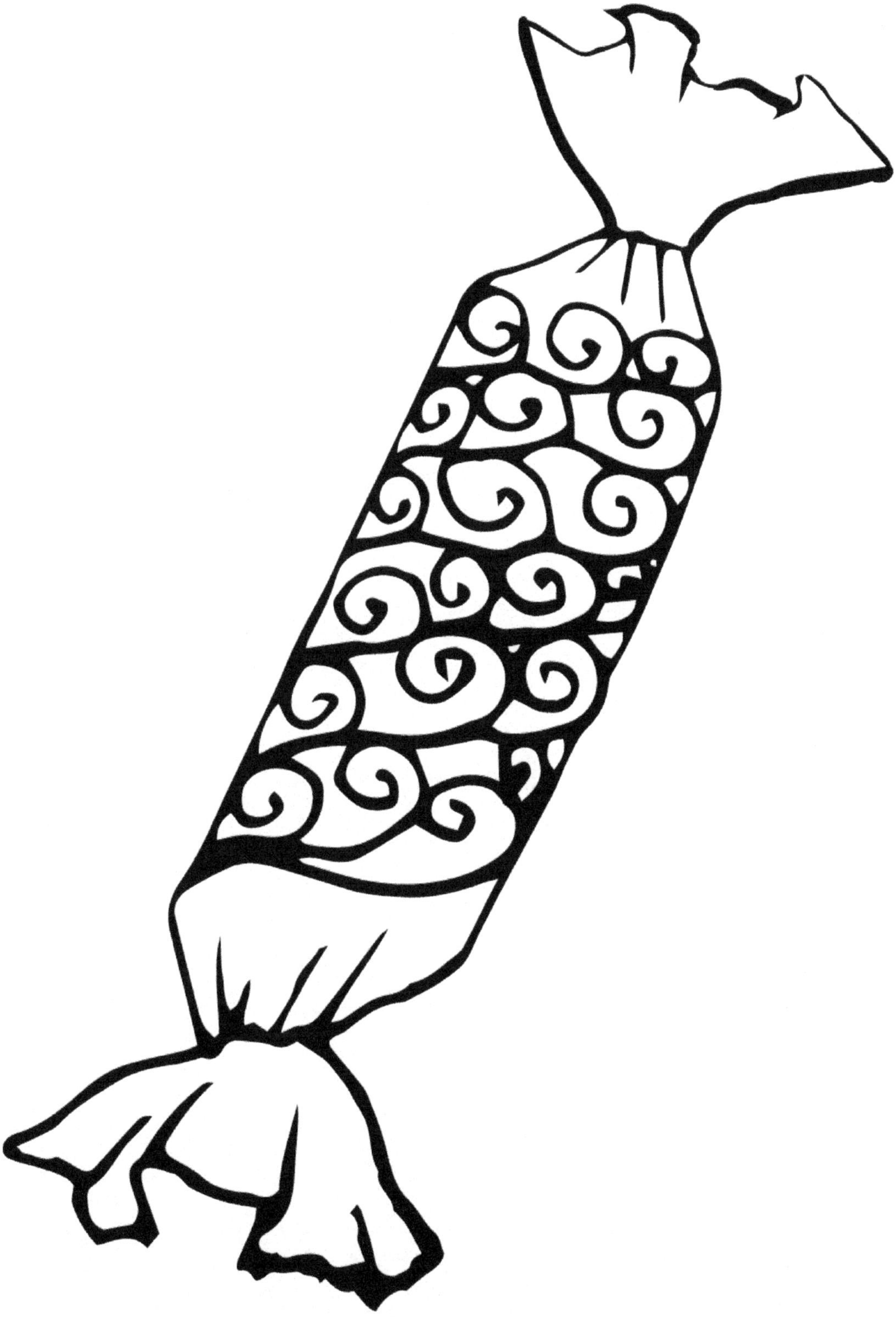

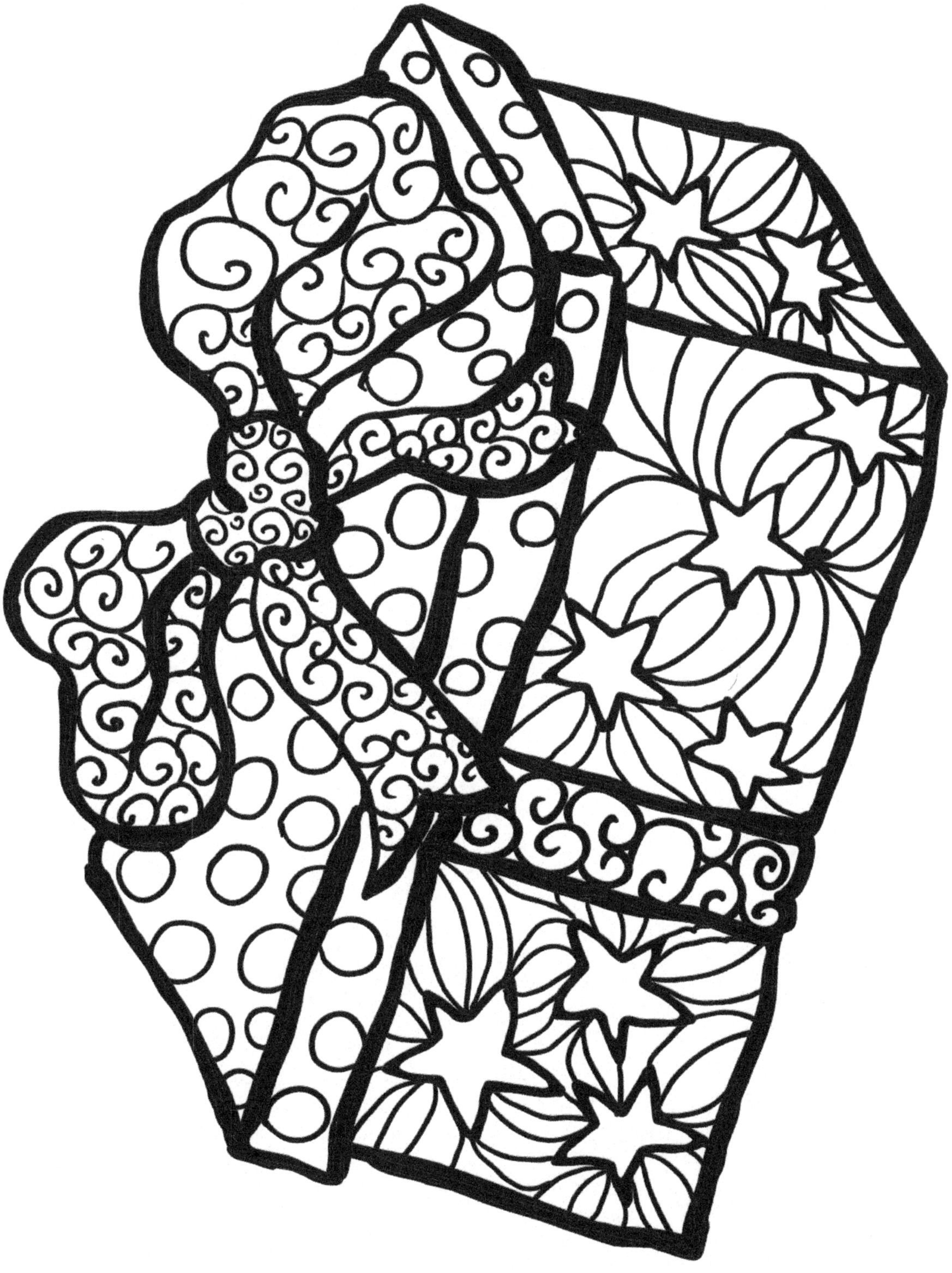

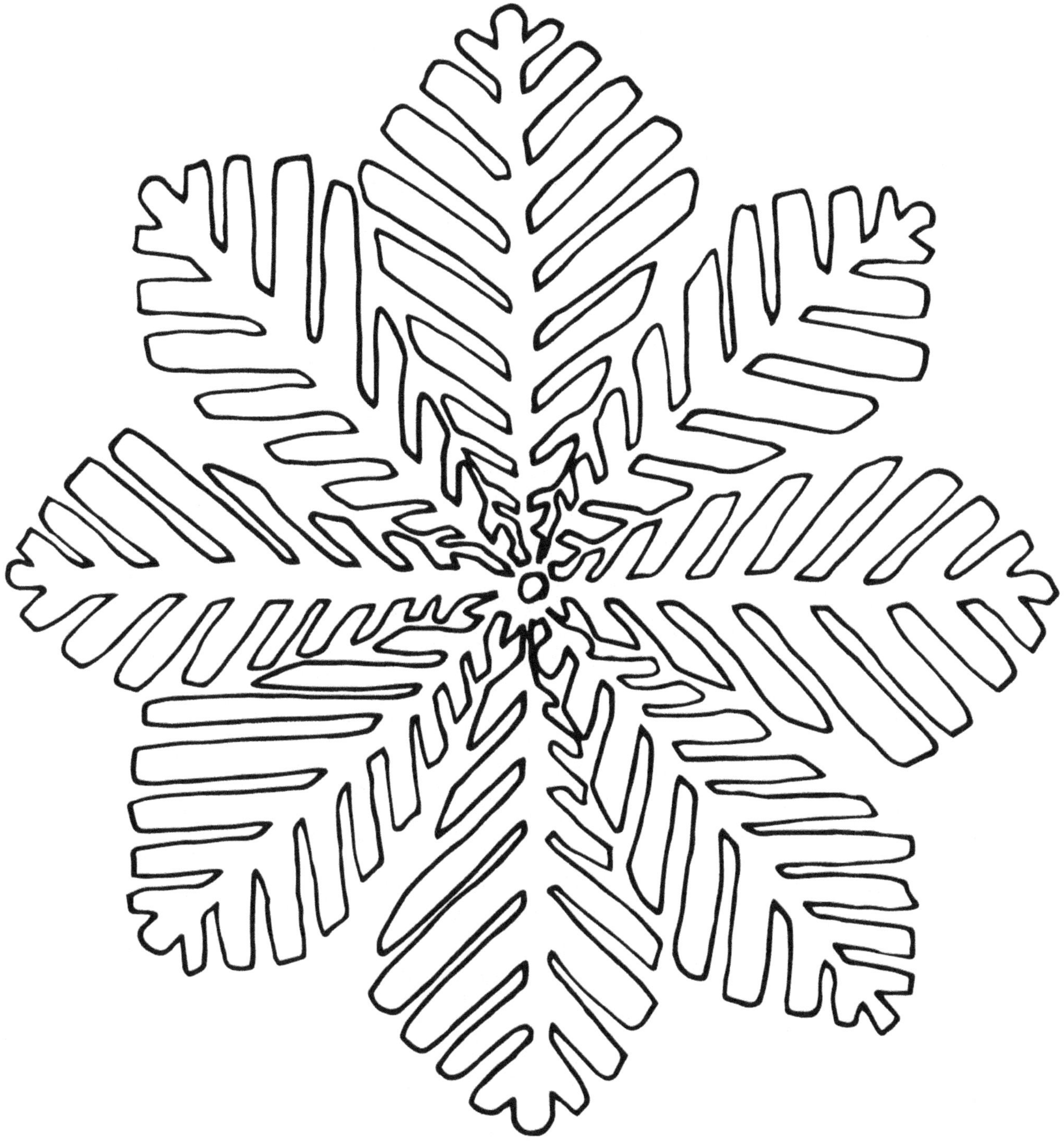

Made in the USA
Las Vegas, NV
26 June 2022

50735736R00057